CW00566150

CONTENTS

FOREWORD

In 1995 Kangaroo Press released a knitting pattern book by Marjory Fainges, *Classic Knits for Boy Dolls*. The book was very well received by home knitters who enjoyed recreating the lovely old patterns for their antique and modern dolls.

And now Marjory has produced another knitting book that is also sure to be a winner, *Classic Knits for Baby Dolls*. The author is an acknowledged world authority on the history of dolls and toys, and has thoroughly researched the history of all of the garments presented here.

The patterns have all been proved by Marjory and will add charm to any baby doll, new or old.

The presentation of this book is lovely, and the diversity of patterns and garments is wide and varied. Baby dolls can have beautiful knitted layettes from these patterns.

The simple instructions of these patterns are suitable for the advanced or beginner knitter and will ensure that your doll will be the envy of all!

Marjory Fainges, an associate editor of the *Australian Doll Digest*, has spent may years researching the history of dolls, especially the history of the Australian doll makers. Other titles to Marjory's credit to date are: *Doll Makers, A History* (1986), *Australian Costume, 1788–1988, for Teen Dolls* (1987), *Antique Dolls of China and Bisque* (1991), *Encyclopaedia of Australian Dolls* (1993) and *Encyclopaedia of Regional Dolls* (1994).

Jacki Brooks
Executive Editor, *Australian Doll Digest*

CLASSIC KNITS FOR BABY DOLLS

Marjory Fainges

Kangaroo Press

Dedicated to all the knitters who just love to knit,
and in particular to make doll's clothes for their own
and other people's dolls.

Acknowledgments

Thanks again to Dorothy and Jane Coleman of the United States for first sowing the seeds for a book such as this; Jacki Brooks (*Australian Doll Digest*) and Helen Whelan, both of New South Wales, Lynn Riddell-Robertson and friend Barbara, both of Victoria, for their encouragement; all the hoarders and lovers of dolls and knitting, particularly those who are meticulous about dressing dolls in the right clothing for their era; Shirleyanne McKay of New South Wales for her help in soliciting some wonderful old patterns from friends; Ross Schmidt and Sue Leighton-White (Sanshi) of Western Australia for their help with old and rare patterns; two wonderful people, Peggy Beer and Joan Arkell of Coffs Harbour, who helped with the proving of the patterns as a double check after I had knitted all the garments and written up the instructions; Gwenda Spencer who kindly loaned some of her collection of dolls to add variety to the photographs. A special thanks to my husband Jim who made some of the props and also cooked some of the meals while I worked on the final manuscript.

First published in Australia in 1996 by Kangaroo Press
an imprint of
Simon & Schuster (Australia) Pty Limited
20 Barcoo Street, East
Roseville NSW 2069

A Viacom Company
Sydney New York London Toronto Tokyo Singapore

Printed in Hong Kong through Colorcraft Ltd

ISBN 0 86417 811 5

10 9 8 7 6 5 4

INTRODUCTION

This, the second book in my series on the dressing of dolls in knitted clothing, has been written for all those who love baby dolls, both girl and boy dolls, whether they be a mother or grandmother wanting to dress a doll for the favourite little girl in their life, or a doll collector with a new and naked acquisition crying out to be dressed in clothing from the right era before it is placed alongside its new companions. One of the first dolls a little girl is given is almost certain to be a baby doll, which is why many doll manufacturers over the last century have made these little images, using such diverse materials as bisque china, celluloid, composition and, in later years, plastic to mimic or characterise a real life baby in many shapes and sizes.

Many of the baby dolls made before the 1960s were made with non-committal features so that the new owner could decide for herself whether the doll was to represent a 'little baby sister or brother', and many dolls' layette patterns were designed to suit this fact. Whether a doll arrives dressed or undressed, the new owner always wants more clothes for it, so that she can continually dress and undress this precious new acquisition. Over the years, of course, many precious pieces of a once pristine baby doll's layette become either badly soiled or sadly misplaced.

As in my first book in this series, *Classic Knits for Boy Dolls*, I have chosen to present knitting patterns suitable for dolls spread over a wide number of years, with patterns originating from the early 1920s through to the late 1940s, and the late 1950s, by permission of Coats Patons. At the same time, because these are 'classic knits', they can be used on baby boy or girl dolls of much later manufacture. I trust that in this book you will find just the pattern you have been looking for to recreate those wonderful remembered moments of long ago.

I hope you get as much enjoyment from knitting these garments as I have, both from researching and making them. Some of your baby dolls can now be attired in a new suit of clothing, instead of wearing a girl's outfit or sitting naked at the back of the cupboard, waiting for the day a pattern for a suitable outfit can be found. Happy knitting.

Proving old knitting patterns

As both the denier size or thickness of the wool ply, and the method of writing knitting pattern instructions, have changed greatly over the years, and as many of the old patterns had mistakes in them (such as the suitability of the pattern to the number of stitches required, or lines of pattern omitted), I have had to prove every one of the patterns in this book before passing them on to two friends, Peggy Beer and Joan Arkell, who kindly and willingly knitted and recorded either smaller or larger versions of many of the patterns.

Altering the size of a pattern

The outfits included here will fit dolls ranging in size from 12.5 cm (5") to 56 cm (22"). Using a combination of garments from different patterns will give an even greater variety. Other outfits are portrayed on dolls that may be of a different size, shape and period, and it is here that my instructions differ from the norm; instead of giving the number of stitches required for a bigger size, I have for simplicity used the difference that a variation in ply and size of needles can give to produce the required sizes for different dolls. Thus with no extra effort, following the examples given in these instructions, clothing for larger or smaller dolls can be made from any of the patterns given, just by adjusting the size of the needles and the wool or yarn used.

If you like a pattern which is too small for your large doll, you can change to 5-ply wool and bigger needles, such as 4 or 4.5 mm (No. 8 or No. 7) (US size 6 or 7), or even larger sized wool and needles. The garment will be much bigger than the original, without having to change the number of stitches and rows. On the other hand, knitting a pattern with 1 mm (No. 16) or finer needles and very fine wool or yarn, such as 1-ply, will give you much smaller finished garments.

This is why the instructions for the patterns are all given in rows, not measured in centimetres or inches. As long as you change the wool or yarn size in proportion with the needle size, the garments will remain in true proportion.

Tension

As some knitters work more loosely (or more tightly) than others, I suggest that you work a trial piece of knitting, 10 sts by 10 rows, to see if you are using the tension recommended in the pattern. If your sample has more stitches or rows than in the pattern, use needles a size smaller; use needles a size larger if your sample has less stitches or rows. If you are an uneven knitter here is a little hint—work your purl rows using a size larger needle than in your knit rows—it works.

Needle sizes

All instructions are given in both metric and imperial measurements, with both Australian/English and US sizes of knitting needles or crochet hooks specified.

Wool or other yarns?

I have used woollen yarn throughout the book, mainly because wool was the medium used in the original patterns. For many of the patterns I have used Bendigo 2-ply and 3-ply fingering wool, which are both available in quite a wide range of both subdued and vibrant colours. This wool is easily available by mail order direct from the Bendigo Woollen Mills in Bendigo, Victoria (they take most credit cards also), or from their overseas distributors (see page 75 for addresses). For other patterns I have used Patons 3-ply Baby Wool or 4-ply Patonyle, both because Coats Patons have kindly given me permission to use patterns from knitting books they have published, and also because these wools are readily available.

In the patterns that I have designed myself, I have used both makes of wool to show the versatility of what can be achieved.

Other wools or yarns, such as those based on nylon, can readily be used. My only suggestion is that you start by making the smallest garment in an outfit to check what difference in size, if any, the different yarn may produce.

Knitting terminology

A very important side to knitting is knowing what all the different terms and abbreviations mean. These are covered fully on page 10. For American knitters I have included a small but concise translation of the differences in crochet terminology, because simple crochet is used for the finish of some garments.

Garment size and your doll

The sizes of the actual garments are given in both metric and imperial measurements, so all you have to do is measure your doll in the appropriate places, regardless of its age, to see whether the garment you have chosen will fit, using the materials given. You may have to change the size of wool and needles, always remembering that *knitted clothes stretch*, and thus can fit a doll bigger than the actual measurements given.

Choosing appropriate patterns

Where possible in the photographs I have used dolls of an age in keeping with the age of the original patterns, but I have also shown more modern dolls wearing the same outfits. As all these patterns are classic patterns for baby dolls, they can really be used on dolls of any age, ranging in size from 12.5 cm (5") to 56 cm (22").

Finishing the garment

To press or not? Pressing is a very important part of giving the finished garment a professional look. If you have used pure woollen yarn, gently press (not iron) each piece of the garment before sewing up, either with a steam iron at a low steam temperature, or using a medium heat iron on a slightly damp cloth placed over the garment piece.

Do not heat-press any garment made from nylon or bri-nylon yarn.

HOW TO KNIT
(or Knitting for Beginners, courtesy of Patons Woolcraft)

Casting-on—making the first loop

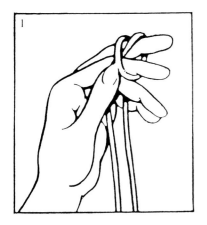 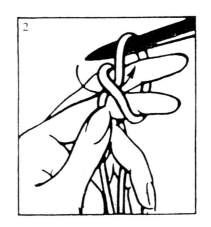 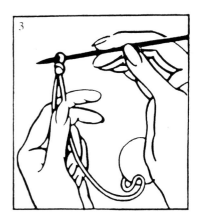

1. Wrap the yarn around the first and second fingers of the left hand.
2. Place point of needle under the front loop and draw back loop through.
3. Withdraw fingers from loop and draw loop up onto needle

Casting-on using thumb and one needle

4. Using the thumb and one needle, and working with a length of yarn sufficient for the required number of sts in your left hand, pass the yarn around the left thumb.
5. Place point of needle beneath the loop on the thumb, drawing loop up slightly.

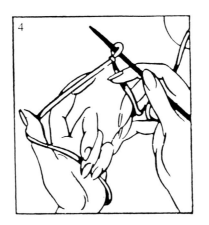 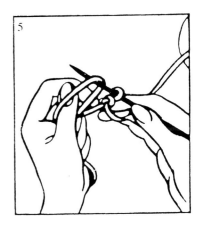

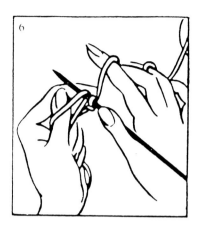
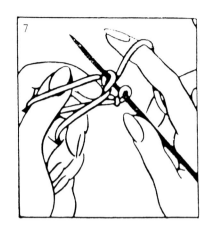
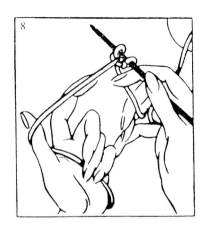

6. Hold yarn from ball in right hand ready to pass around the point of the needle.
7. Wrap yarn from ball around the point of the needle and draw through loop on thumb.
8. Draw up stitch on needle, pull both ends of yarn firmly, and repeat from step 1 until sufficient stitches have been cast on.

Points to watch:
- An even cast-on is essential to good knitting.
- Avoid casting-on too tightly, otherwise edge will not hang properly.
- This form of casting-on does not necessitate knitting into the back of the cast-on stitches.
- This method can be used for all general purposes.

Casting-on—using two needles

Make a loop (following diagrams 1 to 3), then place the point of the right-hand needle through the loop on the left-hand needle. Holding the yarn in the right hand, wrap the yarn around the point of the right-hand needle and draw the yarn through the loop on the left-hand needle, forming a second loop. Place this loop onto the left-hand needle (diagram 9). Now place the point of the right-hand needle *between the two loops on the left-hand needle.* Wrap the yarn around the end of the right-hand needle (diagram 10) and draw a loop between the two loops on the left-hand needle. Place this loop onto the left-hand needle. Put the point of the right-hand needle between the first and second loops on the left-hand needle (counting from the point). Repeat until required number of stitches have been cast on.

Points to watch
Keep the stitches on the left-hand needle near to the point. The yarn should come *over* the first finger of the right hand, *under* the second, *over* the third and *under* the fourth. The yarn should pass easily through the fingers, but should be held firmly to maintain an even tension.

Knitting a stitch
Hold the needle containing the cast-on stitches in the left hand. Insert the right needle from left to right through the first loop, pass the yarn around the point of the right-hand needle, draw a new loop through and, retaining this loop on the right-hand needle, slip the first loop off the left-hand needle (diagram 11).

In plain knitting the wool or yarn is always held at the back of the work. More than one row of knitting stitch creates the pattern known as garter stitch (diagram 12).

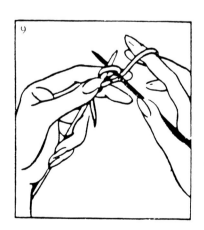
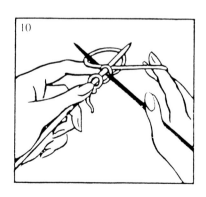
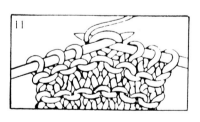
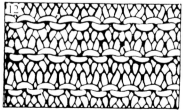

Purling a stitch

Holding the yarn or wool to the front of the work (this is essential when purling), insert the right hand needle from right to left through the first loop on the left-hand needle, pass the yarn around the point of the right-hand needle, draw the loop so formed through stitch onto right-hand needle and drop stitch off left-hand needle. Repeat this action across row (diagram 13).

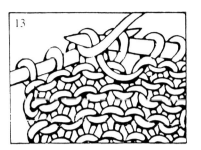

Stocking stitch

By knitting one row and purling the next row a plain smooth pattern is created—this is known as stocking stitch or st st. The side facing you when you work the knit row is usually the right side of the work. Thus the purl side will be the wrong side (unless otherwise stated in the pattern). See diagram 14.

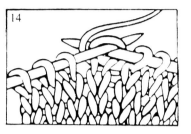

Casting off

Knit the first two stitches, *insert the point of the left-hand needle from left to right through the first of these two stitches, slip this stitch over the second one, that is, take it off the right-hand needle, thus leaving one stitch on the right-hand needle (diagram 15).

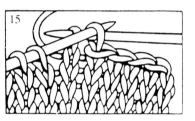

Knit the next stitch and repeat from * until only one loop remains. Break off the yarn and draw the end through the loop of the last stitch. Thread yarn through a yarn needle and darn it neatly into the work.

Important Unless otherwise stated, the edge formed by the cast-off stitches should be as elastic as the remainder of the garment.

When casting off at the beginning of a row (e.g. at the armholes) remember that if 6 sts are cast off, for example, 7 will be needed and used in order to cast off the 6th. This 7th st, therefore, has not been disposed of and must be included in the number of stitches left on the row, and must be counted as the 1st of such stitches.

Tension

The simplest method of measuring tension is to cast on 20 sts using the size of needle and the yarn specified in the pattern (over smooth fabric), knit a square and press lightly. Check the tension by placing a measuring tape along the stitches, marking 2.5 cm (1") with pins and counting the exact number of stitches within the measured length.

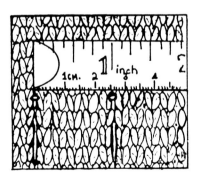

USEFUL INFORMATION

Wool thicknesses

Australian	American
2-ply	2-ply fingering
3-ply	3-ply fingering
4-ply	4-ply fingering
5-ply	

Knitting needle sizes

Metric (mm)	Imperial	American
2.0	14	0
2.5	13–12	1
3.0	11	2–3
3.5	10	4
3.75	9	5
4.0	8	6
4.5	7	7
5.0	6	8
5.5	5	9
6.0	4	10
6.5	3	—
7.0	2	10½
7.5	1	—

Crochet hooks

Metric (mm)	Imperial	American
2.0	14	B/1
2.5	12	C/2
3.0	10	D/3
3.5	9	E/4
4.0	8	F/5
4.5	7	G/6
5.0	6	H/8
5.5	5	I/9
6.0	4	J/10
7.0	2	—

Abbreviations and terminology

* *	repeat instructions between * *
****	refer back to previous section of pattern
alt	alternate
beg	beginning
C	contrast, or lesser colour used in two-colour knitting
dec	decrease—work 2 sts tog to form 1 st
g	gram/s
garter st	work every row in knit stitch
inc	work twice into st to make 2 sts
in	inch(es)
k	knit
m1	make a stitch by placing wool over needle before the next st
MC	main colour used in two-colour knitting
mm	millimetre
ms	moss stitch—work k1, p1, alternately in following rows to give a broken rib effect; usually worked on an uneven no. of stitches.
no.	number
oz	ounce/s
p	purl
psso	pass the slipped stitch over
rep	repeat
rib	usually either k1, p1, or k2, p2, normally worked on an even no. of stitches, repeated to end of row
rib	in the case of garter st, the number of raised rows showing on one side of knitting
sl or sl st	slip the stitch onto needle
st/s	stitch/es
st st	stocking st—working one row in knit st and following row in purl st
tog	working 2 sts together to form 1 st
turn	reverse the way of knitting by working back on the needle just worked
wl fwd	bringing wool to front of work, before working next st, thus making a st; used in patterns and for small buttonholes

Handy hints

1. Knit through back of stitch on all cast-on stitches, using the two-needle method, to give a firm edge, particularly when this method has been used for making a buttonhole.
2. When picking up a stitch, pick up and knit before transferring it onto other needle.

Equivalent crochet terms

Australian/European		American
ch (chain)	=	ch (chain)
sl st (single crochet)	=	sl st (slip st)
dc (double crochet)	=	sc (single crochet)
tr (treble)	=	dc (double crochet)

Old knitting books

Some Australian readers may have old Patons knitting books which include patterns for dolls' clothes. Coats Patons have supplied the years of publication but advise that these books are now *out of print*, and cannot be obtained from the company or its outlets.

Book No. C.3	Published before 1950, reprinted 1950
C.4	Reprinted 1954
C.5	Published 1953, reprinted 1955
C.8	Published 1955, reprinted 1957
C.12	Published 1958
C.13	Published 1959
C.14	Published 1960
C.18	Published 1963
C.23	Published 1970
C.26	Published 1971
C.28	Published 1972
C.38	Published 1979

Care of woollen garments

It takes only a little effort to give knitted garments the care they deserve, especially those made of natural fibres such as pure wool. Make the care regular and you will be rewarded with fresh, new looking clothes for a lifetime.

2-ply, 3-ply and 4-ply wool fingering, and other pure woollen yarns
Warm hand wash only in approved detergent.
Do not rub.
Do not bleach.
Warm rinse well—rinsing is essential.
Normal spin.
Do not tumble dry.
Dry flat and protect from direct sunlight.
Warm iron.
If drycleaning is required, P.50°C is the highest temperature needed.

Baby wool
Read the instructions as many baby wools are now machine washable.
Warm machine wash, short gentle cycle in approved detergent.
Do not rub.
Do not bleach.
Warm rinse well—rinsing is essential
Normal spin.
Do not tumble dry.
Dry flat—protect from direct sunlight
Warm iron
(Instructions courtesy Bendigo Woollen Mills.)

AMBER *Illustrated on page 18*

This pretty little set, knitted in 3-ply and adapted from Weldon's Practical Knitter, *143 series, is easily and quickly made. The coat, bonnet and leggings, just like those a baby of the 1920s would have worn, are worked in a broken moss stitch pattern; the vest and knickers are worked in stocking st.*

Although the pattern originated in the 1920s, it could be adapted to fit many of the hard plastic dolls of the 1950s and 1960s by using a thicker ply wool and larger needles.

Materials

50 g (2 oz) 3-ply baby wool for the coat, bonnet and leggings
25 g (1 oz) white 3-ply baby wool for the vest and knickers
Pair 2.75 mm (12) (US 2) knitting needles
Fine crochet hook
1 m (1 yd) narrow baby ribbon
3 small buttons for jacket

Measurements

Jacket Shoulder to hem	10 cm	(4")
Width around at underarm	20 cm	(8")
Width around hem	23 cm	(9")
Sleeve seam	3 cm	(1¼")
Leggings Waist	18 cm	(7")
Waist to crutch	6.5 cm	(2½")
Inside leg to sole	5 cm	(2")
Outside leg to ankle	10 cm	(4")
Length of foot	4 cm	(1½")
Bonnet Face edge	11.5 cm	(4½")
Depth to back	6 cm	(2½")
Vest Shoulder to hem	8 cm	(3¼")
Width around at underarm	15 cm	(6")
Sleeve seam	1.25 cm	(½")
Knickers Waist	15 cm	(6")
Waist to crutch	6 cm	(2¼")
Inside leg	3 cm	(1¼")
Outside leg	9 cm	(3½")

Tension

10 sts to 2.5 cm (1") over st st; 13 rows to 2.5 cm (1") over st st.

Work 20 rows in st st.
25th row: Cast on 7 sts (for sleeve), knit to end.
26th row: Cast on 7 sts (for sleeve), purl to end (42 sts).
Work 6 rows in st st.
33rd row: k14, p14, k14.
34th row: p14, k14, p14.
Repeat the last 2 rows once.
37th row: k14 (slip these sts onto a safety pin), cast off 14 sts, knit to end.
38th row: Purl.
Work 4 rows in st st. Slip these 14 sts onto a safety pin. Break off wool.
Replace the first 14 sts onto needle, and rejoin wool at neck edge, purl to end.
Work 4 rows in st st.
43rd row: k14, cast on 14 sts, slip sts from safety pin to spare needle (needle point towards neck edge), and knit these sts (42 sts on needle).
44th row: p14, k14, p14.
45th row: k14, p14, k14.
46th row: Repeat 44th row.
Work 6 rows in st st.
53rd row: Cast off 7 sts, knit to end.
54th row: Cast off 7 sts, purl to end.
Work 20 rows in st st.
Work 4 rows in garter st. Cast off.

To make up
Press lightly on wrong side, following instructions on page 6. Sew up side seams, and work a picot edging around neck and armholes.

Vest

Using 2.75 mm (12) (US 2) needles and white wool and commencing at the lower edge, cast on 28 sts, and knit 4 rows in garter stitch (knitting into the back of each cast-on st to give a firmer edge).

Knickers

Using white wool and 2.75 mm (12) (US 2) needles, commence at the waist by casting on 60 sts.
Work 6 rows in k2, p2 rib.
Work 24 rows in st st.

31st row: k30, (slip these sts onto a safety pin for right leg), k30.

32nd row: Purl.

***33rd row:* k2 tog, knit until 2 sts remain, k2 tog.

34th row: Purl.

Repeat last 2 rows 4 times (20 sts).

Work 2 rows in st st.

Work 6 rows in k2, p2 rib. Cast off***

Transfer sts from safety pin.

Purl 1 row.

Repeat from *** to *** for left leg.

To make up

Press as for vest, then sew up leg seams and back seam.

Coat

With coloured wool and 2.75 mm (12) (US 2) needles, commence work at the top of the back, casting on 24 sts.

Knit 1 row (knitting into back of each cast-on st).

1st row: k1, (inc in each of the next 4 sts), k14, (inc in each of next 4 sts), k1.

2nd row: Purl.

3rd row: k2, (inc in each next 2 sts), k2, (inc in each of next 2 sts), k16, (inc in each next 2 sts), k2, (inc in each of next 2 sts), k2.

4th row: Purl.

5th row: k3, (inc in each of next 2 sts), k4, (inc in each of next 2 sts), k18, (inc in each next 2 sts), k4, (inc in each of next 2 sts), k3.

6th row: Cast on 4 sts, purl to end.

7th row: Cast on 4 sts, k16, (inc in each of next 2 sts), k6, (inc in each of next 2 sts), k20, (inc in each of next 2 sts), k6, (inc in each of next 2 sts), k8.

8th and each alternate row: k4, purl until 4 sts remain, k4.

9th row: k9, (inc in each next 2 sts), k8, (inc in each of next 2 sts), k22, (inc in each of next 2 sts), k8, (inc in each of next 2 sts), k9.

11th row: k10, (inc in each of next 2 sts), k10, (inc in each of next 2 sts), k24, (inc in each of next 2 sts), k10, (inc in each of next 2 sts), k10.

13th row: k11, (inc in each of next 2 sts), k12, (inc in each of next 2 sts), k26, (inc in each of next 2 sts), k12, (inc in each of next 2 sts), k11.

15th row: k12, (inc in each of next 2 sts), k14, (inc in each of next 2 sts), k28, (inc in each of next 2 sts), k14, (inc in each of next 2 sts), k12.

16th row: k4, purl until 4 sts remain, k4 (96 sts).

17th row: k14, slip next 18 sts onto a safety pin (for first sleeve), cast on 4 sts for underarm, knit across next 32 sts, slip next 18 sts onto a safety pin (for second sleeve), cast on 4 sts for underarm, k14 (68 sts on needle).

18th row: k4, purl to last 4 sts, k4.

19th row: k4, *k2, p2, repeat from * to last 4 sts, k4.

20th row: k4, purl to last 4 sts, k4.

21st row: k4, *p2, k2, repeat from * until 4 sts remain, k4.

22nd row: As 20th row.

23rd row: As 19th row.

24th row: As 20th row.

25th row: k4, work in pattern for 12 sts, (inc in each of next 2 sts), work 32 sts in pattern, (inc in each of next 2 sts), work 12 sts in pattern, k4. (When inc keep pattern over pattern.)

26th row: As 20th row.

Work 6 rows in pattern.

33rd row: k4, work 14 sts in pattern, (inc in each of next 2 sts), work 32 sts in pattern, (inc in each of next 2 sts), work 14 sts in pattern, k4 (76 sts).

24th row: As 20th row.

Work 8 rows in pattern.

Work 9 rows in garter st. Cast off.

Sleeves (both alike)

Transfer sts from safety pin to needle, join in wool.

Cast on 2 sts, k2, p2 alternately to end, cast on 2 sts.

2nd row: Purl.

3rd row: p2, k2 alternately to end.

4th row: Purl.

5th row: k2 tog, work in pattern until 2 sts remain, k2 tog.

6th row: Purl.

7th row: Work in pattern.

8th row: Purl.

Repeat last 4 rows once.

Work 6 rows in garter st. Cast off.

To make up

Sew up sleeve seams of coat.

Work the following crochet edge along neck of coat: Join wool at edge of right front, 1 dc into sts, *3 ch, miss a stitch, 1 dc into next sts, repeat from * around neck. Fasten off.

(US readers: 1 sc into st, *3 ch, miss a stitch, 1 sc into next sts, repeat from * around neck.)

Crochet a chain, thread through holes formed at neck, make two tiny ball tassels and attach these to end of chain.

Leggings

Commencing at the top edge, cast on 32 sts, and work 6 rows in k2, p2 rib.

7th row: *k2, p2, repeat from * to end.

8th row: Purl.

9th row: *p2, k2, repeat from * to end.

10th row: Purl.

Repeat last 4 rows 6 times.

35th row: Work 16 sts in pattern, slip them onto a safety pin, work remaining 16 sts in pattern.**

36th row: Purl.

37th row: k2 tog, knit in pattern to end.

38th row: Purl.

Repeat last 2 rows 7 times (8 sts).

53rd row: Work in pattern to last st, k2 into st.

54th row: k2 into first st, purl to end.

Repeat last 2 rows twice more (14 sts).

Work 4 rows in pattern.

63rd row: Work in pattern to last 2 sts, k2 tog.

64th row: p2 tog, purl to end.

Repeat last 2 rows twice more.

69th row: k2 into first st, work in pattern to end.

70th row: Purl.

Repeat last 2 rows 7 times (16 sts).

Work 2 rows in pattern, and slip sts onto a safety pin.

Return to stitches held on other safety pin, transfer to needle, making sure point of needle is towards the centre. Join in wool and purl to end of row.

37th row: Work in pattern until 2 sts remain, k2 tog.

38th row: Purl.

Repeat last 2 rows 7 times (8 sts).

53rd row: k2 into first st, work in pattern to end.

54th row: Purl until 1 st remains, k2 into last st.

Repeat last 2 rows twice (14 sts).

Work 4 rows in pattern.

63rd row: k2 tog, work in pattern to end.

64th row: Purl until 2 sts remain, p2 tog.

Repeat last 2 rows twice.

69th row: Work in pattern until 1 st remains, k2 into last st.

70th row: Purl.

Repeat last 2 rows 7 times (16 sts).

Work 2 rows in pattern.

87th row: Work in pattern, slip sts from safety pin to needle (point towards centre), work in pattern to end.

88th row: Purl.

Work 26 rows in pattern.

Work 6 rows in k2, p2 rib.

Cast off.

Bonnet

Cast on 32 sts, work 4 rows in garter st (knitting into back of each cast-on st).

Work 2 rows of k2, p2 rib.

7th row: Knit.

8th row: Purl.

9th row: Purl.

10th row: *k2, p2, repeat from * to end.

11th row: Purl.

12th row: *p2, k2, repeat from * to end.

13th row: Purl.

Repeat last 4 rows 4 times.

30th row: *k4, sl 1, k2 tog, psso, repeat from * until 4 sts remain, k4.

31st row: Purl.

32nd row: k3, *sl 1, k2 tog, psso, k2, repeat from * until 6 sts remain, sl 1, k2 tog, psso, k3.

33rd row: Purl.

34th row: k2, *sl 1, k2 tog, psso, repeat from * until 2 sts remain, k2 (8 sts).

Cut thread, leaving enough wool to thread on needle. Take thread through sts, and draw up tightly.

Turn back front of bonnet, make 2 small ball tassels, sew one each side of bonnet, sew on ribbon strings.

AMETHYST *Illustrated on page 17*

A lovely little set of dress, bonnet, bootees and panties, for either a 36–41 cm (14–16") doll or a 28–30.5 cm (11–12") doll. The set is ideal for both the composition dolls of the 1940s and the early hard plastic dolls of the 1950s. The pattern has been adapted from an early Australian Home Journal *pattern (with a pair of bootees added), and is quick to knit in the larger size as it is done in 4-ply. I used Thorobred wool, a product of New Zealand, but any good 4-ply baby wool will do. Just check your tension by knitting the smallest garment to see if the finished product is the same. Using 3-ply baby wool will give you a smaller set of garments. If you wish to make them even smaller, use 2-ply wool and 2 mm (14) (US 0) needles.*

LARGER DOLL (36–41 cm/15")

Materials

100 g (4 oz) Thorobred 4-ply baby wool (or other good 4-ply baby wool)
Pair 3.25 mm (10) (US 4) knitting needles
1 small decorative button for the neck of the dress (or you can use ribbon ties)
4 m (4½ yds) narrow baby ribbon
1 m (1 yd) wider ribbon for the bonnet

Measurements

Dress Shoulder to hem	21 cm (8¼")
Width around at underarm	38 cm (15")
Sleeve seam	7.5 cm (3")
Bonnet Face edge	23 cm (9")
Depth to back	10 cm (4")
Panties Waist	28 cm (11")
Waist to crutch	10 cm (4")
Leg seam	7.5 cm (3")

Tension

6 sts to 2.5 cm (1") over moss st; 10 rows to 2.5 cm (1") over moss st.

SMALLER DOLL (28 cm/11")

Materials

75 gm (3 oz) Cleckheaton 3-ply Baby Wool (or other good baby wool)
Pair 2.75 mm (12) (US 2) knitting needles
1 small decorative button for the neck of the dress (or you can use ribbon ties)
3 m (3¼ yds) narrow baby ribbon for the dress cuffs, panties and bootees
1 m (1 yd) wider ribbon for the bonnet

Measurements

Dress Shoulder to hem	18 cm (7")
Width at underarm	33 cm (13")
Sleeve seam	6 cm (2½")
Bonnet Face edge	20 cm (8")
Depth	7.5 cm (3")
Panties Waist	23 cm (9")
Waist to crutch	8 cm (3¼")
Leg seam	6 cm (2½")
Bootees Length of foot	4 cm (1½")

Instructions for smaller size given inside square brackets [ ].

Tension

8 sts to 2.5 cm (1") over moss st; 14 rows to 2.5 cm (1") over moss st.

Pattern (used throughout)

1st row: k1, *k3, m1, k3 tog, m1, rep from * to last st, k1.
2nd row: Purl.
3rd row: k1, *m1, k3 tog, m1, k3, rep from * to last st, k1.
4th row: Purl.
These 4 rows form the pattern.

Dress (knitted in one piece)

With 3.25 mm (10) (US 4) needles and 4-ply wool [2.75 mm (12) (US 2) and 3-ply wool], cast on 134 sts and work 8 rows in moss st.
Work 8 rows in pattern (2 patterns).
Work 8 rows in moss st.
Work 12 patterns (48 rows).

1st row: k2, *k2 tog, k1, rep from * to end (90 sts).
2nd row: Purl.
3rd row: k1, *k1, m1, k2 tog, rep from * to last 2 sts, k2.
4th row: Purl.
5th row: (k1, p1,) 24 times, turn.
6th row: (p1, k1) 24 times.
These 48 sts are for the front yoke.

Left front yoke
1st row: (k1, p1) 12 times, turn.
2nd row: (p1, k1) 12 times.
3rd row: k2 tog, (k1, p1) 11 times.
4th row: (p1, k1) 10 times, p1, k2 tog.
5th row: k2 tog, (k1, p1) 10 times.
6th row: (p1, k1) 9 times, p1, k2 tog.
7th row: k2 tog, (k1, p1) 9 times.
8th row: (p1, k1) 8 times, p1, k2 tog.
9th row: (k1, p1) 9 times.
10th row: (p1, k1) 9 times.
11th row: As 9th row.
12th row: Cast off 3 sts, moss st to end.
Continue in moss st for 8 rows. Cast off.
Join wool at front opening of right front yoke and work to correspond, reversing shapings.

Back yoke
With right side of work facing, join wool to remaining 42 sts, and work 4 rows in moss st.
5th row: k2 tog, moss st to last 2sts, k2 tog.
Repeat 5th row twice (36 sts).
Continue in moss st for 13 rows.
Next row: Cast off 12 sts, work in moss st to end.
Next row: Cast off 12 sts and work in moss st to end.
Cast off remaining 12 sts.

Collar
With a fine back seam sew up shoulder seams.
Using 3.25 mm (10) (US 4) needles if using 4-ply [2.75 mm (12) (US 2) needles if using 3-ply], carefully pick up and knit 49 sts around neck, and work 10 rows in moss st. Cast off.

Sleeves
Cast on 32 sts in wool and needles you are using, and work 2 rows in moss st.

Work 2 complete patterns and then the first two rows of pattern.
Work 22 rows in moss st.
Next row: Cast off 3 sts, work in moss st to end.
Repeat last row until there are 14 sts left on needle. Cast off.
Work another sleeve the same.

To make up
Press lightly following instructions on page 6. Sew up side of skirt with a flat seam. Join sleeve seams with a flat seam and set sleeves into position in armholes, using a fine seam. Sew on button at neck and make a buttonhole loop to correspond. Thread ribbon through waist and wrists.

Bonnet

Cast on 56 sts with the wool and needles you are using, and work 4 rows in moss st.
Work 4 complete patterns (16 rows).
Next row: *moss st 13, inc once in next st, rep from * to end (60 sts).
Work 11 rows in moss st.
To shape the crown:
1st row: *moss st 8, k2 tog, rep from * to end.
2nd and every alternate row: Moss st.
3rd row: *moss st 7, k2 tog, rep from * to end.
5th row: *moss st 6, k2 tog, rep from * to end.
7th row: *moss st 5, k2 tog, rep from * to end.
9th row: *moss st 4, k2 tog, rep from * to end.
11th row: *moss st 3, k2 tog, rep from * to end.
13th row: *moss st 2, k2 tog, rep from * to end.
Break off wool and run end through remaining sts. Fasten off securely.

To make up
Press following instructions on page 6. Using a flat seam, join crown for 2.5 cm (1") from secured end. Attach ribbons to front edge of bonnet.

AMETHYST Two lovely dolls of the late 1940s–early 1950s show off their brand new outfits. The 28 cm (11") doll was made by Moldex Melbourne, and the larger doll is a 40.5 cm (16") post-World War II Japanese celluloid character baby doll, marked Oriental/Japan/No.55/Pat.No/380851. This doll still has her original price of 24/- ($2.40) marked in pencil on her back. Their toy is a small wooden swan rocker suitable for a dollshouse. Pattern on page 15.

AMETHYST

AMBER Dressed just as the doll owner's baby sister would have been in the 1920s, in a charming 3-ply outfit of bonnet, jacket, leggings, vest and knickers, this little 23 cm (9") bisque-headed baby doll (3–2/o) is nursing a little Schuco monkey. Pattern on page 12.

PERIDOT All rugged up to face the winter chill, a lovely old 30.5 cm (12") composition doll waits patiently for her young owner to take her for an outing to show off her nice new clothes: white bonnet, jacket, dress, vest, combinations and shoes. Pattern on page 46.

Opposite **DIAMOND** Just like a real baby, Marjory's childhood doll, a 48.5 cm (19") Japanese 'Baby Blue Eyes' sleeping-eyed celluloid, holds her pulled-off bootee in one hand. In her other hand she holds a lovely small googley-eyed all-bisque doll that has been in Marjory's family for over seventy years. Pattern on page 28.

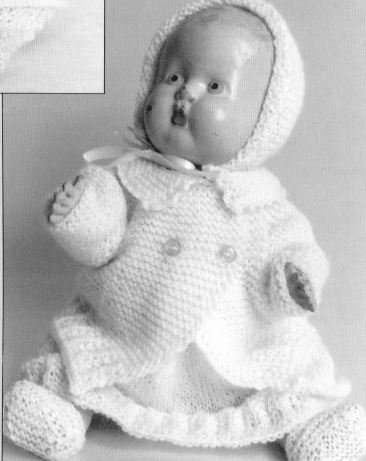

DIAMOND

CARNELIAN

JADE

Panties

Cast on 38 sts with wool and needles you are using and work 3 rows in k1, p1 rib.
4th row: k1, *m1, k2 tog, rep from * to last st, k1.
Work 3 more rows in k1, p1 rib.
Work 3 complete patterns (12 rows).
1st row: moss st 4, k1, k2 tog, m1, (work as 3rd row of pattern to last 4 sts), (starting with k1) moss st 4.
2nd row: moss st 4, purl to last 4 sts, moss st 4.
3rd row: moss st 8, k2 tog, m1, (work in pattern to last 8 sts), moss st 8.
4th row: moss st 8, purl to last 8 sts, moss st 8.
5th row: moss st 12, (work in pattern to last 12 sts), moss st 12.
6th row: moss st 12, purl to last 12 sts, moss st 12.
7th row: moss st 16, k3, m1, k3 tog, m1, moss st last 16 sts.
8th row: moss st 16, p6, (starting with p1) moss st 16.
Work 4 rows in moss st.
Shaping for legs:
1st row: k2 tog, moss st to last 2 sts, k2 tog.
Repeat 1st row until 14 sts remain. Cast off.
Work another half the same.

To make up
Press following instructions on page 6. Sew up side edges and between the legs. Thread a ribbon through holes at waist.

Bootees

Cast on 26 sts with wool and needles you are using, and rib 4 rows.
Work 2 patterns (8 rows).
Moss st 6 rows.
K2 tog each end of row in next and every alt row until 12 sts remain.
Break off wool and thread through remaining 12 sts. Secure firmly and sew up seam.
Work another bootee the same.
These bootees may look a little funny before they are lightly pressed, but fit the foot very well.

CARNELIAN The 25 cm (10") hard plastic Cherub doll, made in Victoria in the 1950s, keeps a wary eye on her small companion, a 16 cm (6¼") composition wire-strung doll made in France which Marjory bought in Paris in 1994. The pair wear the same outfit, with the larger doll's outfit knitted in 3-ply baby wool. The smaller doll (who is sitting in an antique ormolou chair made in Germany) has her outfit knitted in 1-ply wool on finer needles. Pattern on page 22.

JADE Looking very chic indeed in her new outfit, this lovely little 14 cm (5½") French Peticollin celluloid doll of the 1930s poses in front of a tomato-red tinplate pram decorated with flowers. Pattern on page 34.

CARNELIAN *Illustrated on page 20*

A lovely set originally designed to fit a 25 cm (10") baby doll, consisting of doll's frock, vest and panties, has been adapted and knitted in 3-ply wool, by kind permission of Coats Patons, with the addition of matching bonnet and bootees which I designed to complement the frock. This outfit, in whatever colour you may choose, is eminently suitable for the many small dolls that were manufactured in hard plastic throughout the world in the 1950s and 1960s, and will look equally well on a doll of today. The smaller size fits a 16 cm (6¼") doll.

LARGE DOLL (25 cm/10")

Materials

25 g (1 oz) white baby wool for the vest and panties
50 g (2 oz) coloured baby wool for the dress, bonnet and bootees
(*or* 75 g (3 oz) if the whole set is knitted in one colour)
Pair 3.25 mm (10) (US 4) knitting needles
Pair 2.75 mm (12) (US 2) knitting needles
2 m (2¼ yds) matching baby ribbon
2 press studs

Measurements

Dress Shoulder to hem	16 cm (6¼")
Around waist	21.5 cm (8½")
Sleeve seam	3 cm (1¼")
Bonnet Face edge	16.5 cm (6½")
Vest Shoulder to hem	8.5 cm (3¼")
Around underarm	16.5 cm (6½")
Pants Around waist	16.5 cm (6½")
Waist to crutch	7 cm (2¾")
Leg seam	3.5 cm (1½")
Bootees Length of foot	3.5 cm (1½")

Tension

7½ sts to 2.5 cm (1") over st st; 10 rows to 2.5 cm (1") over st st.

SMALL DOLL (16 cm/6¼")

Materials

1 small ball 1-ply wool in main colour
1 small ball 1-ply wool in white for undies
Pair 2 mm (14) (US 0) knitting needles
2 m (2¼ yds) fine ribbon
2 small pearl beads (for buttons)

Measurements

Dress Shoulder to hem	11 cm (4¼")
Around waist	15 cm (6")
Sleeve seam	2 cm (¾")
Bonnet Face edge	10 cm (4")
Vest Shoulder to hem	5.5 cm (2¼")
Around underarm	11 cm (4½")
Pants Around waist	12 cm (4¾")
Waist to crutch	4.5 cm (1¾")
Side seam	2.5 cm (1")
Bootees Length of foot	2.5 cm (1")

Tension

11 sts to 2.5 cm (1") over st st; 15 rows to 2.5 cm (1") over st st.

Frock

Front

Using coloured wool, and 3.5 mm (10) (US 4) needles, cast on 55 sts.
1st and 2nd rows: Knit.
3rd row: Knit.
4th row: k1, purl to last st, k1.
Repeat 3rd row once, then 4th row three times.
Proceed as follows:
***1st row:* k2, * wl fwd, k3, wl fwd, k1, rep from * to last st, k1.
2nd row: k1, purl to last st, k1.
3rd row: k3, * sl 1, k2 tog, psso, k3, rep from * to end of row.
4th row: As 2nd row **
Repeat from ** to ** seven times.
Decrease for waist: k1, * k2 tog, rep from * to end of row.
Next row: Knit.
Ribbon row: *k1, wl fwd, k2 tog, rep from * to last st, k1.
Next row: Knit ***

Work 4 rows in st st.
Cast off 4 sts at beg of next 2 rows.
Work 6 rows in st st.
Neck: k6, cast off 8 sts, k6.
Work 7 rows on each group of 6 sts for the shoulders.
Cast off.

Back
Work as for front to ***
Next row: k15, turn.
Next row: k2, p12, k1.
Rep these 2 rows once.
Keeping k2 (back opening) edge correct, cast off 4 sts at beg of next row, then work 13 rows in st st.
Cast off.
Rejoin wool to sts on needle, cast on 2 sts for underlap and, knitting these 2 sts on every row, complete to match other half of back.

Sleeves
Cast on 16 sts.
1st row: Knit.
2nd row: (k1, inc in next st) seven times, k2 (23 sts).
Work in patt as given from ** to ** for front, three times.
Cast off loosely.
Work another sleeve to match.

Neckband
Sew up shoulder seams.
With right side of work facing, knit up 38 sts around neck.
Knit 1 row. Cast off.

To make up
Press lightly following instructions on page 6. Sew up side and sleeve seams. Stitch sleeves in position. Attach press-studs to back opening. Thread matching ribbon through holes at waist.

Bonnet

With coloured wool and 3.5 mm (10) (US 4) needles, beginning at face edge, cast on 39 sts.
Knit 4 rows.
Repeat the four rows of pattern ** to ** 5 times.
Knit 1 row.
Next row: Purl until 2 sts remain, p2 tog (38 sts).
To shape the crown:
1st row: k5, (k2 tog, k4) 5 times, k1, k2 tog.
2nd and all alternate rows: Purl.
3rd row: k4, (k2 tog, k3) 5 times, k1, k2 tog.
5th row: k3, (k2 tog, k2) 5 times, k1, k2 tog.

7th row: k2, (k2 tog, k1) 5 times, k1, k2 tog (14 sts).
9th row: (k2 tog) 7 times.
Cut wool, leaving a long end to thread through the remaining 7 sts. Draw up tightly and secure with a back stitch, then join up the back seam for 4 cm (1¾"). Stitch ribbon ties at each side of bonnet.

Vest

With white wool and 3.5 mm (10) (US 4) needles, cast on 26 sts.
Work 4 rows in k1, p1 rib.
Work 14 rows in st st.
Work 2 rows in garter st.
Continuing in garter st, cast off 5 sts at beginning of next 2 rows.
Work 4 rows in garter st.
Next row: k3, cast off 10 sts, k3.
Work 17 rows on each group of 3 sts.
Next row: k3, cast on 10 sts, k3 (other shoulder strap).
Continue working, first in garter st, then in st st, to match other half of vest.
Press lightly following instructions on page 6. Join side seams.

Panties

With white wool and 3.5 mm (10) (US 4) needles, and commencing at waist, cast on 26 sts.
Work 2 rows in k1, p1 rib.
Next row: k1, * rib 2, wl fwd, k2 tog, rep from * to last st, p1.
Work 3 rows in rib.
Work 10 rows in st st.
Cast off 4 sts at beg of next 2 rows.
Dec once at each end of needle in every row until 6 sts remain. Work 2 rows. Cast off.
Work another piece the same.
Join side seams.

Leg bands
With right side of work facing, knit up 24 sts around the leg.
Work 1 row in k1, p1 rib. Cast off in rib.
Work second leg band the same.
Join the 6 sts and leg bands.
Thread elastic (or ribbon if you prefer) through holes at waist.

Bootees

Using coloured wool and 2.75 mm (12) (US 2) needles, begin at the top edge of the leg and cast on 21 sts.
Knit 2 rows.
Work 4 rows in st st.
Ribbon slot row: k1, (m1, k2 tog) 10 times.
Purl 1 row.
Now divide the sts for the instep as follows:
Knit 13, turn, p5, turn, (leaving 8 sts unworked at each side).
Work 6 rows in st st on the centre 5 sts.

Next row: Purl the 5 instep sts, pick up and knit 4 sts from row ends on left side of the instep, then knit 8 sts left unworked on this side.
Next row: k17, pick up and p4 sts from row ends on opposite side of instep, then k8 sts left unworked at this side (29 sts).
Work 6 rows in garter st.
Cast off.
Work another bootee the same. Press the bootees following instructions on page 6. Join the leg and underfoot seams. Thread ribbon through slots at ankles.

Spring-cleaning in the Moon.

CORAL *Illustrated on page 37*

A complete set of knitted woollies for a 48 cm (19") baby doll, adapted from the Australian Home Journal Santa Claus Supplement, *December 1937. The set comprises dress, petticoat, panties, vest, bonnet and bootees. The garments can easily be adjusted for a smaller doll by using smaller needles and making the items shorter or, for a larger doll, using bigger needles and adding a little more length where necessary.*

Materials

75 g (3 oz) 2-ply Bendigo knitting wool
Pair 3.75 mm (9) (US 5) knitting needles
4 m (4½ yds) narrow baby ribbon
2 m (2¼ yds) 1.5 cm (½") ribbon for dress and bonnet
1 m (1 yd) pale contrasting ribbon for petticoat trim

Measurements

Dress Shoulder to hem	28 cm (11")
Waist measurement	40 cm (16")
Sleeve seam	6 cm (2½")
Petticoat Shoulder to hem	25.5 cm (10")
Waist measurement	36 cm (14")
Neck to hem	22 cm (9")
Bonnet Face edge	22.5 cm (9")
Front to back	11.5 cm (4½")
Vest Shoulder to hem	18 cm (7")
Underarm measurement	30 cm (12")
Neck to hem	14 cm (5½")
Panties Waist measurement	34 cm (13")
Waist to crutch	14 cm (5½")
Leg seam	10 cm (4")
Bootees Length of foot	7 cm (2¾")

Tension

6 sts to 2.5 cm (1") over st st; 10 rows to 2.5 cm (1") over st st.

Dress

Commencing at lower edge, cast on 128 sts and knit 1 row; then work pattern as follows:
1st row: k2, (wl fwd, k2 tog) 3 times, k1, (k2 tog, wl fwd) 3 times, * k1, (wl fwd, k2 tog) 3 times, k1, (k2 tog, wl fwd) 3 times, repeat from * to last st, k1.
2nd and every alternate row: k1, purl to last st, k1.
3rd row: *k3, (wl fwd, k2 tog) twice, wl fwd, k3 tog, (wl fwd, k2 tog) twice, wl fwd, repeat from * to last 2 sts, k2.
5th row: k4, (wl fwd, k2 tog) twice, k1, (k2 tog, wl fwd) twice, *k5, (wl fwd, k2 tog) twice, k1, (k2 tog, wl fwd) twice, repeat from * to the last 3 sts, k3.
7th row: k5, wl fwd, k2 tog, wl fwd, k3 tog, wl fwd, k2 tog, wl fwd, *k7, wl fwd, k2 tog, wl fwd, k3 tog, wl fwd, k2 tog, wl fwd, repeat from * to the last 4 sts, k4.
9th row: k6, wl fwd, k2 tog, k1, k2 tog, wl fwd, *k9, wl fwd, k2 tog, k1, k2 tog, wl fwd, repeat from * to last 5 sts, k5.
11th row: k7, wl fwd, k3 tog, wl fwd, *k11, wl fwd, k3 tog, wl fwd, repeat from * to last 6 sts, k6.
13th row: Repeat row 9.
15th row: Repeat row 7.
17th row: Repeat row 5.
19th row: Repeat row 3.
20th row: k1, purl to last st, k1.
These 20 rows form the pattern. Repeat full pattern 3 times more.
Next row: k1, k2 tog all along row (reducing to 86 sts).
Next row: Purl.
Work ribbon hole rows as follows:
1st row: k1, *wl fwd, k2 tog, repeat from * to last st, k1.
2nd row: k1, purl to last st, k1.

Yoke

Left back
1st row: k8, (k1, p1) 6 times, turn.
2nd row: (k1, p1) 6 times, k8.
Repeat these 2 rows 10 times more, then cast off 8 sts at beginning of next row and work on remaining sts for 4 rows. Cast off.

Front
Join wool at underarm and cast off 5 sts, then *(k1, p1) 6 times, k12, (k1, p1) 6 times, turn and repeat from * 19 times.
Neck and shoulders:
Next row: Work 12 sts, turn and work 5 rows on these 12 sts. Cast off.
Rejoin wool to neck edge, cast off 12 sts, work remain 12 sts.
Work 5 rows on these sts. Cast off.

Right back
Join wool at underarm and cast off 5 sts, then work remaining sts to correspond with left back.

Sleeves
Cast on 22 sts, and knit 3 rows.
Next row: Knit twice into every st (44 sts).
Work the 20 rows of pattern as given for frock, and cast off loosely.

To make up
Join up centre back seam of frock from bottom to ribbon holes. Sew in sleeves, placing seam at underarm.
Crochet a dc (US sc) edging down both sides of remaining back edge, working two small buttonholes (using 4 ch) on one edge. Crochet an edging around neck, *3 ch and 1 tr into same st, miss 2 sts, 1 dc, repeat from * all around. (US: work *3 ch and 1 dc into same sts, miss 2 sts, 1 sc.)

Petticoat

Cast on 53 sts and knit 1 row.
1st row: k2, m1, k3, *sl 1, k2 tog, psso, k3, m1, k1, m1, k3. Repeat from * to last 8 sts, sl 1, k2 tog, psso, k3, m1, k2.
2nd and every alternate row: k1, purl to last st, k1.
3rd row: *k3, m1, k2, sl 1, k2 tog, psso, k2, m1. Repeat from * to last 3 sts, k3.
5th row: k1, k2 tog, m1, k1, m1, k1, *sl 1, k2 tog, psso, k1, m1, k1, m1, sl 1, k2 tog, psso, m1, k1, m1, k1. Repeat from * to last 8 sts, sl 1, k2 tog, psso, k1, m1, k1, m1, k2 tog, k1.
7th row: k1, m1, k1, m1, sl 1, k2 tog, psso, m1, *sl 1, k2 tog, psso, m1, k1, m1, k1, sl 1, k2 tog, psso, k1, m1, k1, m1. Repeat from * to last 8 sts, sl 1, k2 tog, psso, m1, sl 1, k2 tog, psso, m1, k1, m1, k1.
8th row: Repeat row 2.
Work 4 rows in st st.
Ribbon rows:
1st row: k2, *wl fwd, k2 tog, repeat from * to last st, k1.
2nd row: k1, purl to last st, k1.
Reduce for bodice by (k2 tog) 5 times, knit to last 10 sts, (k2 tog) 5 times.

Bodice
1st row: (k1, p1) 8 times, k10, (k1, p1) 8 times.
Repeat this row 17 times.
Next row: (k1, p1) 6 times. Turn and work 8 rows on these 12 sts. Cast off.
Rejoin wool to neck, cast off 18 sts, and work the last 12 sts. Turn and work 8 rows, cast off.
Work second half the same.

To make up
Press carefully, join up side and shoulder seams, leaving an opening for armholes from 6 rows above lace holes.
Work an edging around armhole to correspond with neck of frock.
Crochet a beading (for ribbon) around neck: 1 tr into edge, *miss 2 sts, 2 ch, 1 tr into next st, repeat from * all round. (US: 1 dc into edge, miss 2 sts, 2 ch, 1 dc into next st, repeat from * all around.)
Thread ribbon through ribbon holes at neck and waist. If you wish, thread ribbon in a pale contrasting colour through ribbon holes just above hem of petticoat.

Panties

Cast on 44 sts and work in k2, p2 rib for 4 rows.
5th row: *k2, wl fwd, k2 tog, repeat from * to end.
Work in ribbing of k2, p2 for 3 rows.
1st row: Knit.
2nd row: k1, purl to last st, k1.
3rd row: k twice into 1st st, k to last st, k twice into last st.
4th row: Repeat row 2.
Repeat these 4 rows until there are 52 sts. Continue without shaping for next 8 rows.
Knit 2 tog at both ends of needle in each alternate row until there are 46 sts, ending with a purl row. Work 2 tog at both ends of needle in every row until there are 18 sts.
Work 2 rows without shaping.
Increase 1 st at both ends of needle in every row until there are 46 sts, then at both ends of every alternate row until there are 52 sts.
Work 8 rows without shaping, then decrease at both ends of the needle in every 4th row until there are 44 sts. Work the ribbing and ribbon holes to correspond with the other side of panties. Cast off loosely in rib.
With right side of work facing pick up 49 sts along leg edge and purl 1 row.
Work lace edging as follows:
1st row: k1, *wl fwd, k2 tog, k1, k2 tog, wl fwd, k1, repeat from * to end of row.
2nd row: k1, purl to last st, k1.
Repeat these last two rows once more, then cast off loosely. Repeat on other leg. Sew up seams and thread ribbon through holes at waist.

Vest

Cast on 43 sts and work 6 rows in k1, p1 rib.
Work 40 rows in st st.

Repeat the 8 pattern rows as given for edge of petticoat.
Next row: (k1, p1) 6 times, turn and work 21 rows (leave on spare needle or large safety pin).
Rejoin wool to neck, cast off 19 sts, and work (k1, p1) 6 times. Work 21 rows on these remaining 12 sts.
22nd row: Rib 12, cast on 19 sts, rib 12 from spare needle. Work 48 rows in st st.
Work 6 rows in k1, p1 rib. Cast off.

To make up
Sew up side seams, leaving an opening each side (from beginning of fancy stitching on front) for armhole. Work around armholes and neck as given for petticoat, then thread ribbon through ribbon holes at neckline.

Bonnet

Cast on loosely 49 sts, and work in ribbing of k1, p1 for 3 rows.
Work the two pattern rows as given for leg of panties twice and cast off loosely.
With right side of work facing you, pick up and knit 58 sts across the last row of k1, p1 ribbing.
Work the 20 pattern rows as given for the dress, then 1st and 2nd row of pattern.
Knit 1 row, then purl back, reducing the sts to 55 by dec at each end and once in the middle of the purl row.
Work 6 rows in st st.
1st row: *k9, k2 tog. Repeat from * to end.
2nd and every alternate row: Purl.
3rd row: *k8, k2 tog, repeat from *
5th row: *k7, k2 tog, repeat from *
7th row: *k6, k2 tog, repeat from *

9th row: *k5, k2 tog, repeat from *
11th row: *k4, k2 tog, repeat from *
13th row: *k3, k2 tog, repeat from *
15th row: *k2, k2 tog, repeat from *
Thread the remain sts onto a darning needle, draw into a small circle and sew crown of bonnet together, nearly to the end of the st st area.
Work a shell edging of crochet, as given for neck of dress, across lace edge at front of bonnet and turn back off face. Attach ribbon to sides of bonnet by forming a small rosette of ribbon at each side.

Bootees

Cast on 31 sts and work the two pattern rows as given for leg of panties 3 times, knitting the last 2 sts tog in 6th row.
7th row: Purl.
8th row: Knit.
Repeat these last two rows 3 times, then 7th row once, and make the ribbon holes as given previously.
Shape instep:
k19 turn, *k8 turn, p8 turn. Repeat from * four times.
Break off wool and sew end in neatly.
With right hand needle pick up and knit 5 sts down side of instep, 8 across toe, 5 down other side of instep and remaining 11 sts.
Knit 8 rows without shaping.
Shape heel and toe:
1st row: k1, k2 tog, k15, (k2 tog twice), k15, k2 tog, k1.
2nd row: k1, k2 tog, k13, (k2 tog twice), k13, k2 tog, k1.
Cast off, decreasing at heel and toe. Sew up seam, turn down lace top and thread ribbon at ankle. Make another bootee the same.

DIAMOND *Illustrated on page 19*

Adapted from a small booklet called Homecraft Economy Series—Instructions No. 318, *printed in England. The booklet featured a set of doll's clothing consisting of coat, dress, bonnet, bootees, vest and panties in 3-ply wool, which was said to make an old doll measuring 45 cm (18") 'look like new'. What made this pattern unusual was the statement that it could be made from 'unpicked wool'. Complete instructions were given on the back of the booklet on how to wash and rewind such wool. Because of this, I would date these instructions either in the bad years of Depression in the 1930s or during World War II when wool was scarce.*

Knowing that unpicked wool is thinner than the original product I decided to make the whole outfit in modern 3-ply baby wool, and thus arrived at the dimensions given in the original pattern.

Materials
8 × 25 g (1 oz) balls 3-ply baby wool
Pair 3.75 mm (9) (US 5) knitting needles
Pair 2.75 mm (12) (US 2) knitting needles
Fine crochet hook (for edgings)
4 m (4½ yards) baby ribbon
5 small buttons

Should you wish to knit the garments separately:
Frock: 3 × 25 g (1 oz) balls   Coat: 2 × 25 g (1 oz) balls
Vest: 1 × 25 g (1 oz) ball   Panties: 1 × 25 g (1 oz) ball
Bootees: Small ball

Measurements

Dress Shoulder to hem	30.5 cm (12")
Around waist	42 cm (16½")
Sleeve seam	4 cm (1½")
Jacket Shoulder to hem	24 cm (9½")
Around underarm	41 cm (16")
Around hem	91.5 cm (36")
Sleeve seam	9 cm (3½")
Bonnet Face edge	26 cm (10¼")
Depth from face edge	12 cm (4¾")
Vest Shoulder to hem	21.5 cm (8½")
Around underarm	30.5 cm (12")
Panties Waist	41 cm (16")
Waist to crutch	14 cm (5½")
Bootee Length of foot	6.5 cm (2½")

Tension
7 sts to 2.5 cm (1") over st st; 10 rows to 2.5 cm (1") over st st.

Frock (front and back alike)

Using 3.75 mm (9) (US 5) needles, cast on 93 sts and work 8 rows in garter st.
1st row: *k1, m1, k2 tog. Rep from * to end of row (this is the pattern row).
Repeat this row 27 times.
Then work 48 rows in st st, ending with a purl row.
Decrease for waist:
k3 tog, *k1, k2 tog, k1, repeat from * to last 3 sts, k3 tog.
Next row: Purl.
Next row (ribbon holes): k3, *k2 tog, m1, k3, repeat from * to last st, k1.
Work 9 rows in st st, ending with a purl row.
Shape armholes:
Cast off 5 sts at beg of next 2 rows, then dec 1 st at both ends of every row until 39 sts remain.
Work 3 rows in garter st.
Work 7 pattern rows.
Work 3 rows in garter st, ending on wrong side of work.
Shape neck and shoulders:
Next row: k14, cast off 11 sts, k to end.
Continuing in st st on the 14 sts left on needle, dec 1 st at neck edge on every row until 7 sts remain. Cast off.
Rejoin wool at neck edge and work second shoulder to match.
Work a second piece of match for other half of dress.

Sleeves
Using 3.75 mm (9) (US 5) needles, cast on 42 sts and work 4 rows in garter st.
Work 12 pattern rows (as given for front).
Work 2 rows in garter st.
Shape top:
Continue in st st and dec 1 st at both ends of every alternate now until 20 sts remain. Cast off. Work another sleeve to match.

To make up

Press all pieces of work lightly on wrong side (following instructions on page 6). Sew both sides of right shoulder together, and left shoulder at armhole edges only. Join side and sleeve seams. Sew sleeves into armholes, easing in any extra fullness at top of sleeve.

Work a simple picot edge around back and front neck edges, starting at front edge of left shoulder: *3 ch, 1 sc into 1st of these ch, 1 dc into next (knit) st, sl st into next st. Repeat all around neck to back edge of left shoulder, then work a row of dc along each edge of shoulder seam, making a loop on the back edge for a button. (US readers: check page 11.) Before finishing right off, check that dress fits over head—if loose, work neck a little tighter; if tight, work picot edging looser. Thread ribbon through waist.

Coat

Using 3.75 mm (9) (US 5) needles, cast on 225 sts and work 8 rows in garter st.

Next row: k3, *k1, m1, k2 tog, repeat from * to last 3 sts, k3.

Repeat last row 49 times.

Decrease for waist: k7, *k2 tog. Rep from * to last 8 sts, k8 (120 sts).

Work 17 rows in garter st, then divide work into back and front sections.

Next row: k25, cast off 10 sts, knit to last 35 sts, cast off 10 sts, knit to end.

Continuing in garter st on these last 25 sts, dec 1 st at armhole edge on every row until 20 sts remain.

**Work 23 rows in garter st, ending at front edge.

Shape neck:

Cast off 6 sts at beg of next row, then dec 1 st at same edge on every row until 7 sts remain. Cast off.

Rejoin wool to 50 sts for back and dec 1 st at both ends of every row until 40 sts remain.

Continue, without shaping work: 31 rows in garter st. Cast off.

Rejoin wool to remaining 25 sts and work to match first side (**working 24 rows to front edge).

Sleeves

Using 3.75 mm (9) (US 5) needles, cast on 42 sts and work 6 rows in garter st.

Work 12 pattern rows as given for lower edge of frock.

Work 22 rows in garter st.

Shape top:

Continue in garter st, dec 1 st at both ends of every alternate row until 16 sts remain. Cast off.

Work another sleeve in the same manner.

To make up

Press following dress instructions. Join shoulder and sleeve seams. Stitch sleeves into armholes. Work a row of picot edging (as given for frock) around edges of coat. Fasten fronts with three buttons and loops. Thread ribbon through waist (using holes made by pattern).

Bonnet

With 3.75 mm (9) (US 5) needles, cast on 69 sts and work 6 rows in garter st.

Work 12 rows of pattern as given for frock.

Work 24 rows in garter st.

Cast off 23 sts at beg of each next 2 rows.

Work 32 rows of garter st on remaining 23 sts.

Next row: k2 tog, repeat to end of row. Cast off.

To make up

Press following instructions for dress. Join sides of back flap to cast-off edges of main part of bonnet.

Work a row of picot edging around edge of bonnet, catching in back as required for a better fit on head.

Vest (worked in one piece)

With 3.75 mm (9) (US 5) needles, cast on 56 sts and work 56 rows in k1, p1 rib.

Shape armholes:

Cast off 3 sts at beg of next 2 rows, then dec 1 st at both ends of every alternate row until 46 sts remain.

Work 8 rows in rib.

Shape neck:

Next row: Rib 8, cast off 30 sts loosely in rib, rib remaining sts.

Continue in rib on last 8 sts for 24 rows, ending at armhole edge.

Break off yarn and leave sts on spare needle.

Rejoin yarn to second set of 8 sts and work 25 rows in rib, ending at neck edge.

Cast on 30 sts, then work in rib across 8 sts from spare needle.

On these 46 sts work 8 rows in rib.

Cont in rib pattern, inc 1 st at both ends of every alternate row until you have 50 sts on needle.

Cast on 3 sts at beg of next 2 rows.

Work 56 rows in rib, and cast off loosely in rib.

To make up

Press following instructions on page 6. Join side seams. Work a row of dc (making sure you keep the dc at same tension as knitting) around neck and armholes. Work a 2nd row around neck edge only, as follows, for ribbon holes: *2 ch, 1 tr into 2nd st from hook. Rep from * all around, then work another round of dc. Thread ribbon through neck holes. (US readers: refer to basic abbreviations on page 11 for your equivalent in crochet.)

Panties (worked in one piece)

With 2.75 mm (12) (US 2) needles, cast on 60 sts and work 4 rows in k1, p1 rib.
Next row (ribbon holes): *rib 2, m1, p2 tog. Rep from * to end.
Work 6 rows in rib.
Change to 3.75 mm (9) (US 5) needles and work in st st for 38 rows.
To shape legs:
Cast off 25 sts at beg of next 2 rows, then work 10 rows on remaining 10 sts for gusset.
Cast on 25 sts at end of next 2 rows, then work 38 rows in st st.
Change to 2.75 mm (12) (US 2) needles and work in k1, p1 rib for 6 rows.
Make ribbon holes in next row as before, then work 4 rows in rib.
Cast off loosely in rib.

Leg bands

With right side of work facing and using 2.75 mm (12) (US 2) needles, pick up and knit the 25 cast-off sts along one side of leg opening, the 10 sts along side of gusset, and 25 sts along cast-on edge of leg. Work 6 rows in k1, p1 rib. Cast off loosely in rib.
Work second leg to match.

To make up

Press following previous instructions. Join side seams. Thread ribbon through waist, or crochet a chain cord with double wool and finish off ends with small tassel.

Bootees

With 3.75 mm (9) (US 5) needles, cast on 35 sts and work 6 rows in garter st.
Next row (ribbon holes): *k3, m1, k2 tog, rep from * to end.
Work 16 rows in st st. Cast off. Work another bootee the same.

To make up

Join side edges. Join lower edges, drawing them up slightly while stitching. Thread ribbon through holes.

GARNET *Illustrated on page 38*

What a wonderful layette to make for your favourite little girl's 41–46 cm (16"–18") baby doll, or to dress that naked doll in your collection. A very versatile outfit, consisting of dress, jacket, bonnet, bootees, singlet and panties, which looks good on any doll manufactured over the last fifty years. Due to the timelessness of its design, the outfit can be made in white or any pretty pastel baby colour.

Materials
75 g (3 oz) 3-ply baby wool of a delicate shade for dress, bonnet, jacket and bootees
25 g (1 oz) 3-ply white baby wool for the singlet and pants (*or* 100 g (4 oz) 3-ply baby wool if knitting the layette in one colour)
Pair 3.25 mm (10) (US 3) knitting needles
Pair 3 mm (11) (US 2) knitting needles
Medium size crochet hook, 2.00 mm (US: A)
4.5 m (5 yds) narrow baby ribbon
1 m (1 yd) wider ribbon for bonnet

Measurements

Dress Shoulder to hem	25.5 cm (10")	
Width around waist	31 cm (12")	
Sleeve seam	3 cm (1¼")	
Bonnet Face edge	23 cm (9")	
Depth to back (after turnback)	10 cm (4")	
Jacket Shoulder to hem	15 cm (6")	
Width around hem	35.5 cm (14")	
Length of sleeve seam	8 cm (3¼")	
Singlet Underarm (unstretched)	23 cm (9")	
Shoulder to hem	14.5 cm (5¾")	
Underarm to hem	8 cm (3¼")	
Pants Waist	27 cm (10½")	
Waist to crutch	11 cm (4¼")	
Side seam	6.5 cm (2½")	

Tension
7 sts to 2.5 cm (1") over st st; 13 rows to 2.5 cm (1") over st st.

Frock

Back
With 3.25 mm (10) (US 3) needles cast on 85 sts and work 5 rows in garter st, then work in pattern as follows.
1st row: k4, *m1, k2 tog, k9, rep from * to last 4 sts, m1, k2 tog, k2.
2nd row: p4, *wrn, p2 tog, p9, rep from * to last 4 sts, wrn, p2 tog, p2.
3rd row: k4, *m1, k2 tog, k1, m1, sl 1, k1, psso, k1, k2 tog, m1, k3, rep from * to last 4 sts, m1, k2 tog, k2.
4th row: As 2nd row.
5th row: k4, *m1, k2 tog, k2, m1, sl 1, k2 tog, psso, m1, k4, rep from * to last 4 sts, m1, k2 tog, k2.
6th row: As 2nd row.
These 6 rows form one pattern.
Continue in pattern until 11 patterns (66 rows) have been worked.
Next row: (k1, k2 tog) 5 times, (k2 tog) 27 times, (k1, k2 tog) 5 times, k1 (48 sts).
Change to 3 mm (11) (US 2–3) and work 3 rows in st st, starting with a purl row.
Armhole shaping:
Continue in st st, and cast off 3 sts at beg of next 2 rows, then dec 1 st at beg of next 4 rows. Work 20 rows in st st.
Shoulder shaping:
Cast off 6 sts at beg of next 4 rows. Cast off.

Front
Work as given for back until armhole shaping is completed, then continue in st st for the next 10 rows.
Neck and shoulder shaping:
Next row: Knit 16, cast off 6, k to end.
Continue on last set of sts and dec 1 st at beg of next 4 alt rows.
Cast off 6 sts at beg of next row and next alt row.
Join wool to inner edge (of neck) and purl 1 row. Work second half of neck/shoulder, dec at opposite ends to first shoulder.

Sleeves
With 3.00 mm (11) (US 2–3) needles, cast on 30 sts and work 5 rows in garter st, then change to 3.25 mm (10) (US 3) needles and work in pattern as given for back until 2nd row of 2nd pattern has been worked. Shape top by casting off 3 sts at beg of next 2 rows, then dec 1 st at beg of next 8 rows.
Next row: k2 tog, k12, k2 tog. Cast off.
Work another sleeve the same.

Matinee jacket

Skirt

With 3.25 mm (10) (US 3) needles, cast on 101 sts and work 5 rows in garter st, then work in pattern with garter st borders as follows:

1st row: k6, *m1, k2 tog, k9, rep from * to last 5 sts, k5.
2nd row: k6, *wrn, p2 tog, p9, rep from * to last 5 sts, k5.
3rd row: k6, *m1, k2 tog, k1, m1, sl 1, k1, psso, k1, k2 tog, m1, k3, rep from * to last 5 sts, k5.
4th row: As 2nd row.
5th row: k6, *m1, k2 tog, k2, m1, sl 1, k2 tog, psso, m1, k4, rep from * to last 5 sts, k5.
6th row: As 2nd row.

These 6 rows form one pattern; continue in pattern until 5th patt has been worked. Change to 3.00 mm (11) (US 2–3) needles and work 4 rows in st st, then divide sts for fronts and back as follows:

Next row: k22, cast off 5 sts, k until you have 45 sts after cast-off, cast off 5 sts, k to end.

Continue on last set of sts for left front, remembering to keep your garter st border as set, and dec 1 st at armhole edge on next 2 alt rows. Continue without shaping for 14 rows (beg with a purl row), thus ending at the front edge.

Neck and shoulder shaping:

Cast off 5 sts at beg of next row, then dec 1 st at beg of next 3 alt rows.

Cast off 6 sts at beg of next row, and 7 sts at beg of next alt row.

With wrong side of work facing you, join wool to 46 sts of back and dec 1 st at beg of next 4 rows. Continue without shaping until you have worked 24 rows from the armhole shaping.

Shoulder shaping:

Cast off 6 sts at beg of next 2 rows, and 7 sts at beg of next 2 rows.

Cast off.

With wrong side of work facing you, join wool to 23 sts of right front and, keeping garter st border as set, work to match left front with all shapings at opposite edges.

Sleeves

With 3.00 mm (11) (US 2–3) needles, cast on 30 sts, and work 5 rows in garter st.

Change to 3.25 mm (10) (US 3) needles and work 5 patterns (30 rows), ending with a 6th row.

Shape top of sleeve as given for frock sleeves. Work another sleeve the same.

Collar

Using 3.00 mm (11) (US 2–3) needles, cast on 74 sts. Work 5 rows in garter st.

1st row: As 1st row of dress.

2nd row: k4, repeat as 2nd row of dress to last 4 sts, m1, k2 tog, k2.
3rd row: As 3rd row of dress.
4th row: k4, repeat as 2nd row of dress to last 4 sts, m1, k2, tog, k2.
5th row: As 5th row of dress.
6th row: k4, repeat as 2nd row of dress to last 4 sts, m1, k2 tog, k2.

Repeat these last 6 rows once. Cast off.

Bonnet

With 3.25 mm (10) (US 3) needles, cast on 63 sts, and work 10 rows in garter st.

Next row: k1, *k2, m1, k2 tog, rep from * to last 2 sts, k2.
Next row: Purl.

Work 5 patterns as given for back of frock.

Shape back as follows:

1st row: (k7, k2 tog) 7 times.
2nd and alternate rows: Knit.
3rd row: (k6, k2 tog) 7 times.
5th row: (k5, k2 tog) 7 times.

Continue to dec in this fashion on every alt row until 14 sts remain.

Knit one row.

Next row: (k2 tog) 7 times. Break off wool and run end through remainings sts, draw up and fasten off securely.

Bootees

Using 3.00 mm (11) (US 3) needles cast on 30 sts and work 5 rows of m st.

Change to 3.25 mm (10) (US 4) needles and work 2 patterns.

Change to 3.00 mm (11) (US 3) needles and work 2 rows in garter st.

Next row: *k1, m1, k2 tog, rep from * to end.

Work 3 more rows in garter st.

Next row: k20, turn.
Next row: k10, turn.

Work in garter st on centre 10 sts for 14 rows.

To work toe:

With right side of work facing you, k the 10 instep sts on your needle. Pick up and knit 10 sts down the left hand side of the instep, k across remaining 10 sts to side of bootee. With wrong side of work facing, k30, pick up 10 sts on the other side of the instep, and k the final 10 sts.

Work 3 rows in garter st then shape for foot as follows:

1st row: k2 tog, k16, k3 tog, k8, k3 tog, k16, k2 tog.
2nd and alt rows: Knit.

3rd row: k2 tog, k13, k3 tog, k8, k3 tog, k13, k2 tog.
5th row: k2 tog, k10, k3 tog, k8, k3 tog, k10, k2 tog.
Knit one row. Cast off.

Vest (knitted in one piece)

With 3.25 mm (10) (US 3) needles, cast on 44 sts and work 4 rows in k1, p1 rib.
Continue working in pattern as follows, until 8 patterns (32 rows) have been worked:
1st row: *k1, p1, rep from * to end.
2nd and 3rd row: As 1st row.
4th row: Knit.
Next row: Cast on 4 sts at beg of next 2 rows.
Work 4 rows without shaping.
Next row: *k1, p1*, rep from * to * 5 times, cast off 28 sts, keeping continuity of pattern, work to end of row.
Continue on last set of 12 sts and work 23 rows without shaping; leave these sts on a spare needle.
Join wool to inner edge of remaining sts (neck edge), and work 23 rows in pattern.
Next row: Working in pattern k1, p1, work 12 sts, cast on 28 sts, then work the 12 sts from the spare needle in k1, p1 pattern.
Work the back part of the vest until it is the same length as the front, remembering to rib the last 4 rows. Cast off in rib.

To make up
Sew up the two side seams. Work a simple edging around the neck as follows: 1 tr, miss 2k sts, 2 ch (US 1 dc, 2 ch) all around neck. You may then thread a narrow length of ribbon through these holes, and tie a bow at the front.

Panties

With 3.25 mm (10) (US 3) needles, cast on 56 sts and work 2 rows in k1, p1 rib.
Next row: *rib 2, wl fwd, k2 tog, rep from * to end.
Work in pattern as given for vest for 16 rows, then work 2 tog at both ends of every row until 18 sts remain.
Work 4 rows without shaping, then inc 1 st at both ends of every row until there are 56 sts on the needle.
Work 16 rows in pattern, then make a row of ribbon holes as given at beginning.
Rib 2 rows. Cast off in rib.

To make up
Press work lightly on wrong side following instructions on page 6.
Work edging around front neck of frock as follows:
Into the first *2 sts work 1 dc (US sc) then work a picot of (1 dc (US sc) into next st, chain 3, then work into first st of ch), rep from * along neck edge. Repeat the same for the back edge.
Join shoulder seams of frock, leaving 2.5 cm (1") open at neck edges. Sew in sleeves, then join side and sleeve seams. You may use ribbon ties at neck edges of shoulder or use snap fasteners.
Join shoulder seams of coat, sew in sleeves, then join sleeve seams. Sew on collar to fit.
As the panties and vest can be made up on either side, pick which side you wish to show, and carefully sew up side seams. Work a picot edging around neck and sleeves of vest if you wish. Thread ribbon through holes of panties' waist. Join back and sole seams of bootees. Sew ties on front of bonnet, and thread narrow ribbon wherever there are ribbon holes.

JADE *Illustrated on page 20*

Adapted from one of the patterns included in Knitted Sets for Dolls, *first published in Melbourne in the 1930s, as an ideal outfit to knit quickly for that special school or church bazaar. Especially suited to the small celluloid doll shown wearing this little outfit, knitted in 2-ply wool, the set consists of dress, bonnet, singlet and panties. It would look just as wonderful on any small doll of any era, and is so quick and easy to knit you will want to make more!*

Materials
25 g (1 oz) 2-ply wool in any pastel shade (I used Bendigo 2-ply)
Pair 3.25 mm (10) (US 3) knitting needles
Pair 2.00 mm (14) (US 0) knitting needles
Fine crochet hook
1.5 m (1½ yds) narrow baby ribbon

Measurements
Dress Shoulder to hem	11 cm (4¼")	
Waist	11.5 cm (4½")	
Width around hem	28 cm (11")	
Sleeve seam	2 cm (⅝")	
Bonnet Face edge	7.5 cm (3")	
Depth to back	4 cm (1½")	
Singlet Shoulder to hem	7.5 cm (3")	
Width around at underarm	11.5 cm (4½")	
Panties Waist	12.5 cm (5")	
Waist to crutch	5 cm (2")	
Leg seam	4 cm (1½")	

Tension
8 sts to 2.5 cm (1") over broken rib; 10 rows to 2.5 cm (1") over broken rib.

Dress

Back
Cast on 41 sts loosely with 3.25 mm (10) (US 3) needles, and knit 4 rows garter st. Then knit in pattern as follows:
1st row: k1, *k2 tog, repeat from * to end of row.
2nd row: Increase by k1 st, then pick up and knit loop between the last st and the next st. Repeat in this fashion to end of row (41 sts).
3rd row: Knit.
4th row: Purl.
Work these 4 pattern rows 8 times. Then reduce sts to 21 by k1, then *k2 tog to end.
Next row (wrong side): Make ribbon holes by k1, (m1, k2 tog) to end.

Next row: Rib k1, p1, repeat to last 2 sts, p2 tog (20 sts).
Work in rib for 3 cm (1¼"). Cast off.

Front
Work the same as the back of the dress until 2.5 cm (1") of ribbing has been worked.
Next row: Rib 6, cast off 8 sts, rib 6.
Rib these 6 sts for 6 mm (¼"). Cast off.
Join wool to other side and work to match.

Sleeves
Cast on 13 sts.
Work 2 rows in garter st, then work the 4 pattern rows twice. Cast off.
Make another sleeve the same way.
Sleeves may be omitted and a crochet edge worked around the armholes.

Singlet

Cast on 22 sts loosely.
Work in k1, p1 rib for 5 cm (2").
Work 6 rows in garter st.
Next row: k7, cast off 8 sts, k7.
Knit 2.5 cm (1") in garter st on these 7 sts (leave on needle).
Join wool to other side and work to match.
Then k7, cast on 8 sts, k7.
Knit 6 rows in garter st, and then 5 cm (2") of ribbing. Cast off.

Panties

Cast on 23 sts.
Knit 2 rows in garter st.
Work the 4 pattern rows 3 times, and then the 1st and 2nd row of pattern.

Change to garter st and k2 tog at each end of every row until reduced to 7 sts.
Knit 6 rows on these 7 sts.
Then increase 1 st at each end of every row up to 23 sts.
Repeat the 4 pattern rows 4 times. Cast off.

Bonnet

Cast on 25 sts. Knit one row.
Knit the 4 pattern rows 3 times, then the 1st and 2nd row of pattern.
Knit 4 rows of garter st.
K2 tog along row and cast off.
Fold in half and sew the cast-off sts together to form back of bonnet.

Bootees

With 2-ply wool and 2 mm (14) (US 0) needles, cast on 21 sts.
Knit 2 rows.
Work 4 rows in pattern as given for frock, then rows 1 and 2 again.

Ribbon slot: k1, *(m1, k2 tog), rep from * to end of row.
Purl 1 row.
Divide the sts for instep as follows:
Knit 13, turn, purl 5, turn.
Work 6 rows in st st on these 5 sts.
Next row: Knit 5 sts, pick up 5 sts along side of instep, knit remaining 8 sts on left hand needle.
Next row: Purl 18 sts, pick up 5 sts along side of instep, purl remaining 8 sts (on left hand needle).
Work 5 rows in st st. Cast off.
Work another bootee the same. Join leg and underfoot seams. Thread ribbon through slots at ankles.

To make up outfit
Sew up seams, leaving space for armholes in both the dress and the singlet, and leave the left shoulder of the dress open. Sew the sleeves in place.
Crochet a tiny edge around the neck of the dress and singlet, and all around the bonnet, drawing the back of the bonnet in slightly.
Make a small loop on one edge of the left shoulder, and sew a small button or pearl bead on the other side.
Make loops and ties and sew to bonnet. Thread narrow ribbon through holes at waist of the dress and panties, and if you wish, the neck of the singlet.

JASPER *Illustrated on page 39*

A delicate but very easily made layette suitable for a 24 cm (9½") baby doll. Knitted in 3-ply baby wool, it comprises bonnet, jacket, dress and bootees knitted in a chosen main colour. For a doll of the 1940s, the vest and panties can be knitted either in the same colour or in off white, or for a more modern doll in white. If you would like to make this outfit for a larger doll, try 4-ply wool and 4 mm (8) (US 6) needles.

Materials

75 g (3 ozs) main colour baby wool
25 g (1 oz) white wool (for undies)
Pair 3.25 mm (10) (US 4) knitting needles
Pair 2.75 mm (12) (US 2) knitting needles
Medium crochet hook
3 m (3¼ yds) baby ribbon
2 small buttons

Measurements

Frock Length	14 cm (5½")	
Around body	21 cm (8")	
Sleeve seam	3 cm (1¼")	
Jacket Shoulder to hem	10 cm (4")	
Around at underarm	26 cm (10¼")	
Sleeve seam	6 cm (2¼")	
Bonnet Face edge	15 cm (6")	
Back to front	7 cm (2¾")	
Vest Shoulder to hem	10 cm (4")	
Around body	18 cm (7")	
Panties Waist to crutch	8 cm (3⅛")	
Around body	18 cm (7")	
Bootees Length of foot	5 cm (2")	

Tension

8 sts to 2.5 cm (1") over st st; 10 rows to 2.5 cm (1") over st st.

Frock (back and front alike)

With main colour wool and 3.25 mm (10) (US 4) needles, cast on 47 sts.
Purl 1 row.
**1st row (right side): k3, *m1, k2 tog, k2, repeat from * to end.
2nd row: k3, *p1, k3, repeat from * to end **
(Note: ** to ** form the 2 pattern rows used throughout.)
Repeat these 2 rows 9 times.
Work 13 rows in st st.
Change to 2.75 mm (12) (US 2) needles.
Dec row (wrong side): p2, *p2 tog, p1, repeat from * to end (32 sts).
Ribbon slot row: k2, *m1, k2 tog, repeat from * to end.
Work 7 rows in st st.
To shape armholes:
Dec 1 st at each end of the needle in next row, and following 3 alternate rows (24 sts).
Work 3 rows in st st.
Next row: k5, cast off 14 sts, k5.
Work 7 rows in st st on the last 5 sts. Cast off.
Rejoin wool to first 5 sts and work 7 rows in st st. Cast off.
Work front exactly the same as the back.

Sleeves
With main colour and 2.75 mm (12) (US 2) needles, cast on 19 sts.

Opposite **CORAL** A lovely 48 cm (19") doll dressed in her new 1930s-type outfit of dress, petticoat, vest, panties, bonnet and bootees. The doll was assembled in the 1930s by Laurie Cohen Company of Sydney, New South Wales, using an A.M. 352/4 bisque head, on his own design cloth body, with Japanese celluloid arms and legs. The doll is holding an Edwardian era bead and wire rattle which has a wooden handle complete with whistle. Pattern on page 25.

Page 38 **GARNET** Looking sweet in her brand new pink outfit is a 38 cm (15") bisque-headed doll with a cloth 'frog' body and German celluloid hands, known as a 'Bye-Lo Baby' (also famous as the 'Million-Dollar Baby'). The marking on the back of her head is C 1923 by/Grace S. Putnam/Made in Germany. Her accessory is a very old wind-up Easter 'trembler' toy—the two birds and the egg tremble when the key is wound. The outfit includes dress, bonnet, matinee jacket, bootees, singlet and panties. Pattern on page 31.

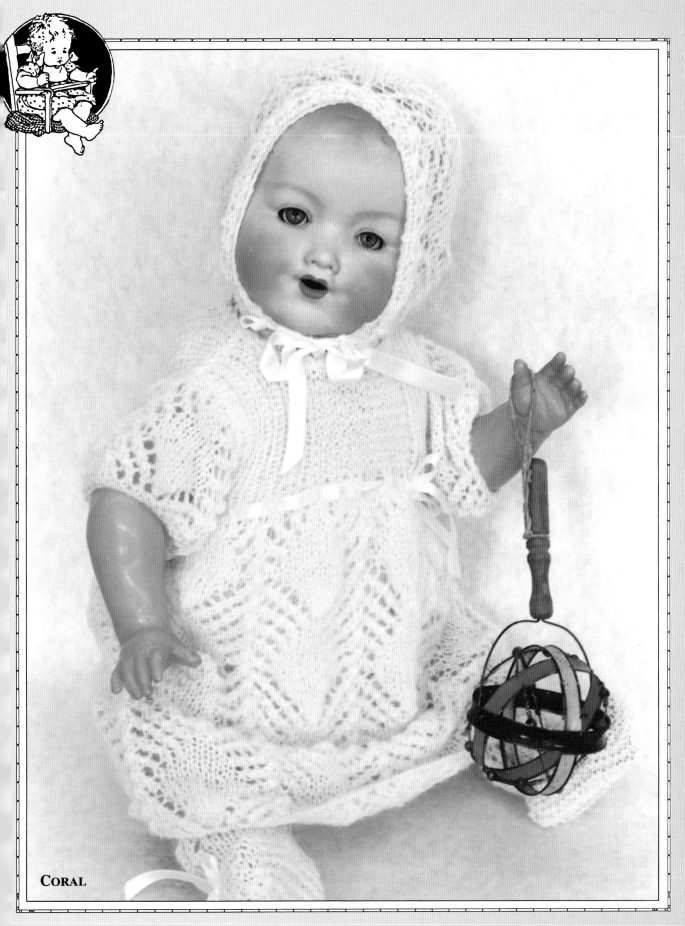

CORAL

GARNET

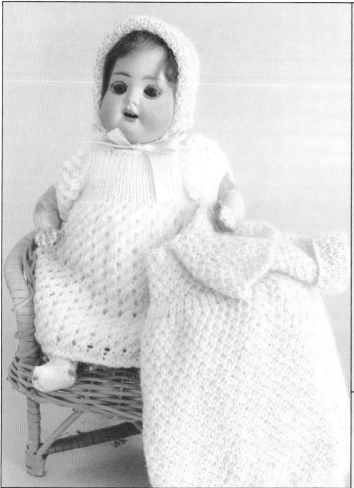

Topaz This lovely layette, from a pattern first published in 1937, is modelled by a charming 23 cm (9") bisque-headed Recknagel baby

R 86 A

9/o.

She is sitting in an old toy cane chair, with her cape-collared coat draped over one chair arm. Her outfit consists of coat, bonnet, dress, slip, panties and vest. Pattern on page 59.

Jasper Safe in the care of a friendly old German Steiff teddy is the 25 cm (10") Hermsdorfer ('Ladybird' trademark) German celluloid doll, dressed in the 3-ply woollen Jasper outfit. Pattern on page 36.

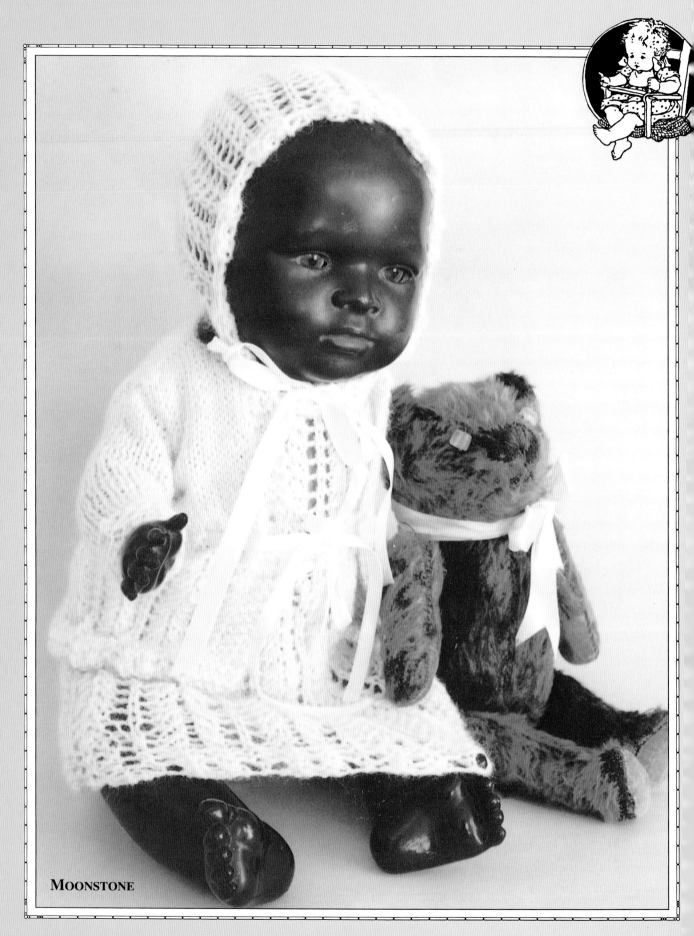

MOONSTONE

Knit 2 rows. Change to 3.25 mm (10) (US 4) needles.
Work 6 rows in st st, then inc 1 st at each end of the next row (21 sts).
Work 5 rows in st st.
Shape sleeve top by dec 1 st at each end of the next row and following 2 alt rows (15 sts).
Cast off.
Work another sleeve in the same manner.

To make up
Press all pieces following instructions on page 6. Join the shoulders at armhole ends only. Set the sleeves into armholes. Join sleeve and side seams.

Neckbands
With right side of dress facing, and using 2.75 mm (12) (US 2) needles, pick up 20 sts around the front edge. Knit 1 row, and cast off. Work the back neckband the same way. Work a button loop on each front shoulder, and stitch a small button to each back shoulder edge to correspond.
If desired work a small picot edging around the hem of the frock. Thread ribbon through ribbon holes at waist.

Coat

Back
Using 3.25 mm (10) (US 4) needles, and main colour, begin at the lower edge by casting on 39 sts.
Purl 1 row.
Work 10 patterns as given for the frock.
Work 4 rows in st st.
Change to 2.75 mm (12) (US 2) needles.
To work armholes:
Continuing in st st, dec 1 st at each end of the next row, and following 4 alt rows (29 sts).
Work 7 rows in st st. Cast off.

Left front
Cast on 23 sts in main colour, using 3.25 mm (10) (US 4) needles.
Purl 1 row.
Work 10 patterns as given from ** to ** for frock back.
Change to 2.75 mm (12) (US 2) needles.
1st row: Knit.
2nd row: k3, purl to end.
Repeat these last 2 rows once.

Shape armholes:
1st row: k2 tog, knit to end of row.
2nd row: k3, purl to end.
Repeat these last 2 rows 3 more times, then the 1st row once again (18 sts).
Work 4 rows in st st, remembering to keep the garter st border at the front edge.
*** Cast off 12 sts for the neck, work to end.
Work 4 rows in st st on remaining 6 sts. Cast off ***

Right front
Work the same as the left front until the 10 patterns (** to **) have been completed.
Change to 2.75 mm (12) (US 2) needles.
1st row: Knit.
2nd row: p20, k3.
Repeat these last two rows once.
Shape armholes:
1st row: Knit until 2 sts remain, k2 tog.
2nd row: Purl until 3 sts remain, k3.
Repeat these last 2 rows 3 times, and then the 1st row again (18 sts).
Work 5 rows in st st, keeping the garter st border as before, then repeat from *** to *** from left front.

Sleeves
Using 2.75 mm (12) (US 2) needles, cast on 17 sts.
Work 4 rows in garter st.
Change to 3.25 mm (10) (US 4) needles.
Work 4 rows in st st.
Continuing in st st, inc 1 st at each end of the next and every following 4th row, until you have 25 sts on the needle.
Work 3 rows in st st.
Shape sleeve:
Dec 1 st at both ends of the next and following 3 alt rows (17 sts).
Cast off.

To make up
Join shoulder seams. Using 2.75 mm (12) (US 2) needles, pick up and knit 16 sts from the right front neck edge, 18 sts from back edge, and 16 sts down left front neck.
Work 1 row in k1, p1 rib.
Ribbon hole row: k2, *m1, k2 tog, k1, repeat from * to end.
Rib one row as before. Cast off in rib.

Bonnet

Using 3.25 mm (10) (US 4) needles, cast on 39 sts with main colour wool.
Purl 1 row.
Repeat the 2 pattern rows as given for back of frock 8 times.
Knit one row.
Next row: k3, purl to last 3 sts, k3.
Work 2 rows in st st, keeping the 3 garter sts border at each end, and k2 tog at end of 2nd row.
Shape crown:
1st row: k5, (k2 tog, k4) 5 times, k1, k2 tog.
2nd and following alt rows: Purl.
3rd row: k4, (k2 tog, k3) 5 times, k1, k2 tog.
5th row: k3, (k2 tog, k2) 5 times, k1, k2 tog.
7th row: k2, (k2 tog, k1) 5 times, k1, k2 tog.
Next row: p2 tog 7 times.
Break off wool, leaving a long end, thread needle and thread through remaining 7 sts. Draw up tight, and fasten securely. Sew back seam to start of pattern area.
If desired work picot edging around the face edge.
Finish off by stitching ribbon ties to each side of bonnet.

Bootees

With 2.75 mm (12) (US 2) needles and main colour, cast of 21 sts.
Knit 2 rows.
Work 4 rows in st st.
Ribbon hole row: k1, *m1, k2 tog, repeat from * to end of row.
Purl 1 row.
Divide sts for instep as follows:
Knit 13, turn, p5 (leaving 8 sts unworked at each side of top of instep).
Work 6 rows in st st on the centre 5 sts.
Next row: Knit the 5 instep sts, pick up and k4 sts down side of instep, k8 sts.
Next row: p17, pick up and p4 sts down side of instep, then purl to end (29 sts).
Work 8 rows in garter st. Cast off.
Work another bootee the same.
Join leg and underfoot seams. Thread ribbon through slots at ankles.

Vest (back and front alike)

Back
Using white wool and 2.75 mm (12) (US 2) needles, cast on 28 sts.
Work 6 rows in k1, p1 rib.
Change to 3.25 mm (10) (US 4) needles, and work 14 rows in st st.
Shape armholes:
Dec 1 st at each end of the next row and following 3 alt rows (20 sts).
Work 3 rows in st st.
Next row: k4, cast off 12 sts, k4.
Work 7 rows in st st on these last 4 sts. Cast off.
Rejoin wool to neck edge, and work 7 rows in st st on these remaining 4 sts. Cast off.
Work front same as back.

To make up
Join shoulder and side seams. Work around neck edge to make ribbon holes: *2 ch, 1 tr, into 2nd st from hook, repeat from * all around neck.
Work 1 row of dc (US sc) around armholes.

Panties (back and front alike)

Using 3.25 mm (10) (US 4) needles and white wool, cast on 8 sts.
Work 4 rows in st st.
Next row (right side): Cast on 11 sts, knit to end.
Next row: Cast on 11 sts, purl to end (30 sts).
Work 18 rows in st st.
Work 4 rows in k1, p1 rib.
Ribbon hole row: k1, *m1, k2 tog, repeat from * until 1 st remains, k1.
Work 3 rows in rib. Cast off.
Work front to match back.
Leg edging: Join side seams. Using 3.25 mm (10) (US 4) needles, pick up 25 sts around leg edge. Cast off.
Work other leg edging to match. Join together at crutch, and thread either ribbon or elastic through ribbon holes.

MOONSTONE
Illustrated on page 40

This little five-piece doll's outfit consisting of bonnet, dress, jacket, leggings and nappy is very versatile. Knitted in 3-ply and adapted from an early 1940s pattern, the outfit is ideal for a girl baby doll up to 43 cm (17") using just the bonnet, dress, jacket and nappy. Should you wish to outfit a boy doll, the bonnet, buttoned jacket and leggings are ideal for a 38 cm (15") doll. Although designed over fifty years ago, this simple design will still suit today's dolls.

Materials
75 g (3 oz) 3-ply wool (I used Bendigo 3-ply) for the girl version
or 50 g (2 oz) 3-ply wool for the boy version
(3-ply baby wool will produce smaller versions of all pieces)
Pair 3.75 mm (9) (US 5) knitting needles
3 small buttons for the jacket
2 press-studs for the dress
1 large safety pin for the nappy
3 m (3½ yds) ribbon
Fine crochet hook

Measurements

Dress Shoulder to hem	23 cm (9")	
Around waist	27 cm (10½")	
Coat Shoulder to hem	16.5 cm (6½")	
Width around hem	35.5 cm (14")	
Sleeve seam	8 cm (3¼")	
Bonnet Face edge	22 cm (8½")	
Depth from turnback	10.5 cm (4¼")	
Nappy Waist length	32 cm (12½")	
Waist to point	22.5 cm (8¾")	
Leggings Waist	23 cm (9")	
Front waist to crutch	13 cm (5")	
Inside leg to ribbon holes	10 cm (4")	
Length of foot	5 cm (2")	

Tension
7 sts to 2.5 cm (1") over st st; 9 rows to 2.5 cm (1") over st st.

Coat

Cast on 99 sts for lower edge. Knit 2 rows.
1st row: k4 for border, (k2 tog, k1, m1, k1, m1, k1, sl 1, k1, psso) 13 times, k4.
2nd row: Knit.
Repeat these 2 rows twice more.

7th row: As 1st row.
8th row: k4, p91, k4.
Repeat the last 2 rows 9 times, then dec for waist:
Next row: k4, (k4, k2 tog) 15 times, k5.
Next row: k4, p76, k4.
Next row: k4, (m1, k2 tog) 38 times, k4.
Next row: k4, p76, k4.
Work 10 rows, keeping the 4 border sts each end and the rest of the work in st st; in the 3rd row work a buttonhole.
Buttonhole row: k2, m1, k2 tog, k to end.
Work 1 row.
Next row: Knit 22 sts, and place on a safety pin.
Knit the next 40 sts for the back, and place the remaining 22 sts on another safety pin.
Working on the 40 sts for the back, dec at the armhole edge at both ends of the next 4 rows.
Work 12 rows straight in st st. Cast off.
With right side facing, place first set of sts onto a needle and join wool at armhole edge.
Continuing with border of 4 sts, dec at armhole edge of the next 4 rows, whilst making a buttonhole as before on the 2nd row.
Continue until you have worked 9 rows, making another buttonhole in the 8th row.
Next row: Cast off 4 sts at beginning of row (neck edge), and 2 sts at beginning of next 2 alt rows.
Purl 1 row and cast off.
Work left front to match, omitting buttonholes, and working decreases in their respective places.

Sleeves
Cast on 14 sts. Knit 2 rows.
Next row: (k2 tog, k1, m1, k1, m1, k1, sl 1, k1, psso) twice.
Next row: Knit.
Repeat these 2 rows, then work 22 rows in st st, increasing at both ends of 1st and every following 4th row, until there are 24 sts on the needle.
Work 5 rows in st st.
Work 2 tog at both ends of next 8 rows. Cast off.
Make another sleeve the same.

To make up
Join shoulder seams. Work 1 row of dc (US sc) around neck edge. Join sleeve seams. Set sleeves in armholes. Stitch three buttons to left front. Thread ribbon through holes at waist.

Dress

Cast on 98 sts.
1st row: (k2 tog, k1, m1, k1, m1, k1, sl 1, k1, psso) 14 times.
2nd row: Knit.
Repeat these 2 rows twice more.
7th row: As 1st row.
8th row: Purl.
Repeat the last 2 rows 20 times.
Next row: (k2 tog, k1, k2 tog, k2) 14 times (70 sts).
Next row: Rib 28, p14, rib 28.
Next row: k1, (m1, k2 tog) 34 times, p1.
Rib 1 row.
Work 12 rows in pattern.

Front
Cast on 2 sts, k2, work 5 patterns on 35 sts.
Place remaining 35 sts on safety pin.
Turn, and cast on 2 sts.
Next row: k2, p35, k2.
Work 6 rows in pattern, with k2 sts at each end of every row.
Next row: k2, work 2 patterns (16 sts on needle), turn.
Work 3 rows on these 16 sts. Cast off.
Place next 7 sts onto a safety pin.
Work 4 rows on remaining 16 sts. Cast off.
Work the back as the front on remaining sts.

To make up
Join shoulder seams, leaving 2.5 cm (1") open at either side of neck. Join side seam and thread ribbon through holes at waist.
Pick up 22 sts (including those on safety pin) round front neck and work 1 row in k1, p1 rib. Cast off loosely in rib. Work back neck border in same way.
Sew a fastener at either side of neck openings.

Bonnet

Cast on 53 sts. Knit 2 rows.
1st row: k2 for border, *(k2 tog, k1, m1, k1, m1, k1, k2 tog into back of st)*, repeat from * to * 6 times, k2.
2nd row: Knit.

Repeat these two rows 15 times.
Work the remaining part of the bonnet in st st as follows:
33rd and 34th rows: Cast off 2 sts, work to end.
35th row: (k3, k2 tog) 9 times, k4.
36th and every alt. row: Purl.
37th row: (k2, k2 tog) 10 times.
39th row: (k1, k2 tog) 10 times.
41st row: k2 tog 10 times.
Cut wool and thread through remaining sts. End off securely, then sew along seam to beginning of pattern. Sew a length of ribbon at end of each front.

Or: If you wish you may pick up and k34 sts along lower edge.
Next row: k1, (m1, k2 tog) 16 times, k1.
Cast off in ribbing. Thread ribbon through holes and tie.

Nappy

This finishes the girl's outfit; it can be used under the boy's leggings if you wish, but you will need more wool.

Cast on 94 sts and st st 2 rows.
1st row: k2, sl 1, k1, psso, k until 4 sts remain, k2 tog, k2.
2nd row: k2, purl to last 2 sts, k2.
Repeat these 2 rows 44 times.
Next row: k2 tog to end. Thread a needle through remaining sts and end off tightly.
Gently press.
With a fine crochet hook (2 mm) (14) (B/1), with right side of work facing, and beginning at the right side of waist, *work 1 dc into next 2 cast-on sts (US sc), miss 1 st, rep from * to other end of waist. This makes the waist edge of nappy nice and firm.

Leggings (optional)

Right leg
Cast on 36 sts and work 2 rows in k1, p1 rib.
3rd row: (k1, m1, k2 tog, p1) to end.
Rib 1 row.
Now proceed in st st.
Next row: k4, turn, p4.
Next row: k8, turn, p8.
Knit 4 sts more in each knit row until 16 sts have been knitted and purled at ends of rows. Work 4 rows straight, then inc at both ends of the following 5th, 9th and 13th rows (42 sts).
Continue in st st for the next 23 rows.
Work 2 tog at both ends of every row until there are 24 sts.

Work straight for 11 rows.
Work 2 rows in k1, p1 rib.
Work ribbonholes as on 3rd row, then rib 1 row.
Next row: k12 for heel, turn, leaving 12 sts on safety pin.
Purl 11, turn, k10, turn, p9, turn, k8, turn, p7, turn, k6, turn, p5, turn, k4, turn, p3.
Knit 4, turn, p5, turn, k6, turn, p7, turn, k8, turn, p9, turn, k10, turn, p11, turn, k12.
Work 3 rows straight in st st.
Dec at both ends of needle in every row until 4 sts remain. Cast off.
Place 12 sts on safety pin onto your knitting needle, rejoin wool and work 4 rows in st st.
Dec at both ends of needle in every row until 4 sts remain. Cast off.

Left leg
Work as right leg for first 4 rows.
Knit 1 row.
Purl 4, turn, and k to end.
Purl 4 sts more each time until 16 sts are purled and knitted. Continue in st st (next row purl), and work as right leg until heel is reached, ending with a purl row.
Knit 12, place these 12 sts on safety pin, k11, turn, p10, turn, and complete this leg to match the right leg.

To make up
Sew back and front seams, also leg and foot seams. Thread narrow baby ribbon through waist and ankles.

Bootees

Begin at the top of the leg edge and using 3.75 mm (9) (US 5) needles, cast on 23 sts. Knit 2 rows.
1st row: k1, *k2 tog, k1, m1, k1, m1, k1, k2 tog (through back of sts), rep from * to last stitch, k1.
2nd row: Knit.
3rd row: As 1st row.
4th row: Purl.
Repeat 3rd and 4th rows twice.
Ribbon row: k1, *m1, k2 tog, rep from * to end of row.
Next row: Purl.
Next row: k15, turn, purl 7.
On these 7 sts work 7 rows in st st, ending with a knit row.
Knit up 8 sts along side of instep, and knit to end of row.
Next row: p23, pick up 8 sts along side of instep and purl to end of row (39 sts).
Work 6 rows in st st.
Next row: k17, k2 tog, k1, k2 tog, k to end of row. Cast off.
Work another bootee the same.

To make up
Sew up the side seam, and underneath the foot. Thread ribbon through ribbon holes.

PERIDOT *Illustrated on page 18*

This knitted trousseau, suitable for any 30–33 cm (12"–13") doll, has been adapted and rewritten from the booklet Australian Home Budget—Toys and Novelties, *dating from the late 1930s–early 1940s. Although shown on a war-time composition doll of the 1940s this outfit would suit celluloid dolls or even their later compatriots made of plastic. To make this outfit for a larger doll, just use thicker ply wool and larger needles.*

Materials

100 g (4 oz) 3-ply wool (I used Bendigo 3-ply) for the dress, coat, combinations, bonnet and shoes (other 3-ply baby wools may produce smaller garments)

25 g (1 oz) 2-ply wool (or one of the cheaper 3-ply baby wools) for the vest

Pair 3.25 mm (10) (US 3) knitting needles

Pair 2.75 mm (12) (US 2) knitting needles

5 small pearl buttons for the coat

6 very small buttons for the dress, combinations and shoes

Measurements

Dress Shoulder to hem	17 cm (6¾")	
Around waist	25 cm (10")	
Sleeve seam	2 cm (¾")	
Coat Shoulder to hem	13 cm (5")	
Around underarm	30 cm (12½")	
Width of hem	32 cm (13")	
Sleeve seam	6 cm (2¼")	
Bonnet Face edge	17 cm (6¾")	
Depth (without turnback)	7 cm (2¾")	
Vest Shoulder to hem	9.5 cm (3¾")	
Around underarm	22 cm (8¾")	
Combinations Shoulder to leg	14.5 cm (5¾")	
Around underarm	25 cm (10")	
Neck to crutch	6 cm (2¼")	
Inner leg seam	6 cm (2¼")	
Shoes Length of foot	4 cm (1½")	

Tension

8 sts to 2.5 cm (1") over st st; 10 rows to 2.5 cm (1") over st st.

Frock

Using 3.25 mm (10) (US 3) needles, cast on 60 sts.

Front

1st row: Knit into back of all cast-on sts.

2nd row: Knit.

3rd row: Knit.

4th row: Knit.

5th row: *k3, p1, repeat from * to end of row.

6th row: k2, p1, *k3, p1, repeat from * to last st, k1.

Repeat 5th and 6th rows 3 times.

13th row: Purl.

14th row: Knit.

15th row: Starting with a knit row, work the following 30 rows in st st.

45th row: *k1, (k2 tog) twice, repeat from * to end of row (36 sts).

46th, 47th and 48th rows: Knit.

Repeat 5th and 6th rows 3 times.

55th row: Purl.

56th row: Knit.

Knit 6 rows in st st, knitting 2 tog at beginning of each row.

Change to 2.75 mm (12) (US 2) needles.

63rd row: Purl.

64th row: Knit.

Work 5 rows in st st.

70th row: p6, k18, p6.

71st row: k6, p18, k6.

Repeat 70th and 71st rows once.

74th row: p6, cast off 18 sts, p6.

Leave the shoulder sts on spare needle for grafting or knitting together, or knit one row on each shoulder piece and cast off.

Back

Work as for front until 62nd row, then divide the sts for right and left side.

Knit to match the front. Work 3 or 4 extra rows on shoulder sts and sew front and back pieces together at shoulders.

Sleeves

With right side of dress facing, pick up 50 sts (25 sts on each side of shoulder seam) on 2.75 mm (12) (US 2) needles and work 6 rows st st.

7th row: k1, k2 tog to end of row.

Knit 6 rows.

14th row: Cast off on wrong side.

Sew up seams. Make 3 small loops at back and sew on 3 tiny buttons to correspond.

Coat

The back and two fronts of this coat are knitted in one piece.

Starting from the bottom of the back with 3.25 mm (10) (US 3) needles, cast on 40 sts.

1st row: Knit into the back of each st.

Knit 3 rows.

Repeat the 5th and 6th rows of the dress pattern 4 times.

Knit 30 rows in garter st (15 ridges).

(Tie a length of coloured thread in the last stitch at both ends of needle in the last row to denote the start of the armholes.)

43rd row: *k1, k2 tog, knit until 3 sts remain, k2 tog, k1.

44th row: Knit*

Repeat from * to * twice (32 sts) (48th row).

Knit 18 rows. (This takes you to the back of the neck.)

67th row: k10, cast off 14 sts, k10.

Knit 9 rows on the 10 shoulder sts.

You now start to knit one front:

76th row: k10, cast on 14 sts (for front).

Knit 17 rows.

94th row: *k1, k2 in next st, knit to end.

95th row: Knit*

Repeat from * to * twice (27 sts).

Knit 30 rows (inc in last st of the 30th row).

Work the 5th and 6th rows of dress pattern 4 times.

Knit 3 rows. Cast off.

Other front:

Rejoin wool at the neck edge of the 10 sts.

Knit 8 rows.

Next row: Cast on 14 sts for front (neck edge), knit across these 14 sts and the 10 sts of shoulder (24 sts).

Knit 18 rows.

Next row: *k1, k twice into next st, knit to end.

Next row: Knit*

Repeat from * to * twice (27 sts).

Knit 30 rows (inc in last st of 30th row).

Work the 5th and 6th rows of dress pattern 4 times.

Knit 3 rows. Cast off.

Coat collar

With wrong side of work facing, pick up 42 sts (leaving 6 sts free at each end of front).

1st row: Knit.

2nd row: *k6, k twice into next st, repeat from *, ending with k7.

3rd, 4th and 5th rows: Knit.

6th row: *k7, k twice into next st, rep from *, ending with k7.

Knit 3 rows.

10th row: *k8, k twice into next st, rep from *, ending with k7.

11th row: Knit.

12th row: *k9, k twice into next st, rep from *, ending with k7.

13th row: Knit.

14th row: Cast off loosely.

Sleeves

Cast on 20 sts, and knit 12 rows.

13th row: *k2, k twice into next st, * rep from * to end of row.

Knit 3 rows.

17th row: k1, k twice into next st at beginning of each row until there are 32 sts.

Knit 6 rows.

Cast off one st at beginning of every row until 24 sts remain.

Cast off.

Work another sleeve the same.

To make up

Sew up shoulder seams and sleeve seams, place sleeves into armholes, and sew in position.

Work dc (US sc) around fronts, leaving 3 tiny spaces to form buttonholes at top. Sew on buttons to match buttonholes.

Shoulder-strap combinations

Right side

With 3.25 mm (10) (US 3) needles, cast on 24 sts.

Knit 1 row.

Repeat 5th and 6th rows of dress pattern twice.

6th row: *k1, k2 into next st, k until 2 sts remain, k2 into next st, k1.

Knit 3 rows*

Repeat from * to * 5 times (36 sts).

To widen for back:

Knit 5, turn, k back, k10, turn, k back, k15, turn, k back, k20, turn, k back.

Knit 22 rows.

Divide sts for front and back.

Front

Knit 18 (place other 18 sts onto a spare needle or knitting safety pin).

Knit 1 row.

Continue in garter st as follows:

Knit 1, k2 tog at beginning of every row until 3 sts remain.

Knit 2 rows. Cast off.

Back

Knit the 18 sts from the spare needle.

Work as for front, until 3 sts remain.

Work 20 rows on these 3 sts for strap. Cast off. Make a loop at the edge.

The left side is worked the same as the right side. Sew up seams. Sew buttons on front and back to keep in position.

Bonnet

With 3.25 mm (10) (US 3) needles, cast on 48 sts.

Knit 2 rows.

Repeat 5th and 6th rows of dress pattern 3 times.

Work 7 rows in st st.

Knit 28 rows.

44th row: *k4, k2 tog, repeat from * to end of row.

45th and alternate rows: Knit.

46th row: *k3, k2 tog, repeat from * to end of row.

48th row: *k2, k2 tog, repeat from * to end of row.

50th row: *k1, k2 tog, repeat from * to end of row.

51st row: Knit.

Break off wool and thread through sts, draw up tightly. Sew up as far as required. Work dc (US sc) around neck of bonnet. Sew on ribbons to tie.

Vest

Using 2-ply wool, and 3.25 mm (10) (US 3) needles, cast on 28 sts.

Knit 30 rows.

Cast off 2 sts at each end for armholes.

Knit 14 rows.

Knit 3, cast off 18 sts (loosely) for neck, k3.

Knit 6 rows on last 3 sts, leave on spare needle. Rejoin wool at neck edge, knit 6 rows.

Knit 3, cast on 18 sts, k3 (from spare needle).

Knit 14 rows.

Cast on 2 sts at each end.

Knit 30 rows. Cast off.

Shoes

With 2.75 mm (12) (US 2) needles, cast on 7 sts.

Knit one row.

Knit 1, k2 into next st at the beginning of each row until you have 21 sts.

Knit 2 rows.

Knit 1, k2 tog at beginning of each row until you have 7 sts (this forms the sole of the foot).

Cast on 5 sts for heel.

Knit, inc at the toe end until you have 15 sts. Cast off 8 sts at the heel end.

On the remaining 7 sts knit 8 rows for instep.

Cast on 8 sts.

Knit, dec at the toe end until 12 sts remain. Cast off. Sew together.

Strap

Cast on 8 sts. Pick up 4 sts from each side of back seam.

Cast on 8 sts.

Knit one row.

2nd row: k1, k2 tog, k until the last 3 sts, k1, k2 tog.

3rd row: Knit.

Cast off. Sew on buttons.

Opposite **RUBY** A late 1940s 46 cm (18") Australian made doll with P.P. New Zealand composition head and lower arms and legs on a cloth body. She is wearing her brand new layette with pretty trimmed bonnet as she shares a secret over a 'cuppa', served from an old marbled glass teapot, with her old friend, a Deans of England teddy bear. Pattern on page 53.

Page 50 **SAPPHIRE** Looking just right, this lovely 46 cm (18") Japanese celluloid doll, manufactured in the early 1930s, has been photographed wearing a knitted set worked in 2-ply wool adapted from instructions first published in 1935. Pattern on page 57.

RUBY

SAPPHIRE

50

TOURMALINE A delightful 33 cm (13") Armand Marseille bisque-headed 'Dream Baby' (351/3K) sits with a rattle over her arm and ponders whether it is cold enough to need the lovely matching jacket set out on the miniature one-sixth scale (1 cm = 6 cm; 2" = 1 ft) wooden dressing table made by Marjory's husband Jim. Pattern on page 62.

TURQUOISE

RUBY *Illustrated on page 49*

Layette is worked throughout in Patons 4-ply Patonyle (you can now use the new Patons 4-ply 'Trends', but please check your tension if using this yarn). The pattern, for dress, jacket, bonnet, singlet, pants and bootees, has been fully corrected and rewritten from its first appearance in a 1947 Australian Home Journal. Because the bonnet was originally designed for the dolls of that time, which had small heads in relation to the size of their bodies, should you wish to make the set for a later doll with a larger head it would be advisable to knit the bonnet on larger size needles to achieve the required size.

Materials

100 g (4 oz) 4-ply Patonyle wool (or other 4-ply wool) in required colour for dress, jacket, bonnet and bootees
50 g (2 oz) 4-ply Patonyle wool in white for singlet and panties
Pair 3.75 mm (9) (US 5) knitting needles
3 m (3½ yds) narrow baby ribbon

Measurements

Dress Shoulder to hem	28 cm (11")
Around underarm	41 cm (16")
Around waist	38 cm (15")
Side seam	20.5 cm (8")
Sleeve seam	7.5 cm (3")
Around hem	61 cm (24")
Jacket Shoulder to hem	18 cm (7")
Around underarm	35.5 cm (14")
Around hem	48 cm (19")
Side seam	10 cm (4")
Sleeve seam	10 cm (4")
Bonnet Face edge	21.5 cm (8½")
Depth from face edge	10 cm (4")
Singlet Shoulder to hem	18 cm (7")
Around underarm	27 cm (10¾")
Side seam	13.5 cm (5¼")
Pants Waist	31 cm (12¼")
Waist to crutch	12 cm (4¾")
Leg seam	9.5 cm (3¾")
Bootee Length of foot	5.5 cm (2¼")
Leg from heel to top	7.5 cm (3")

Tension

6 sts to 2.5 cm (1") over st st; 10 rows to 2.5 cm (1") over st st.

Jacket

Cast on 131 sts and knit 6 rows.
7th row: Knit.
8th row: k4, p to last 4 sts, k4.
9th row: k4, p to last 4 sts, k4 (right side).
10th row: k4, p to last 4 sts, k4.
11th row: Knit.
12th row: Repeat row 8.
13th row: k6, *k2 tog, m1, k1, m1, sl 1, k1, psso, k1. Repeat from * to last 5 sts, k5.
14th row: Repeat row 8.
15th row: k5, k2 tog, *m1, k3, m1, sl 1, k2 tog, psso. Repeat from * to last 10 sts, m1, k3, m1, sl 1, k1, psso, k5.
16th row: Repeat row 8.
17th row: Repeat row 13.
18th row: Repeat row 8.
19th row: Repeat row 15.
20th row: Repeat row 8.
21st row: Knit.
22nd row: k4, p to last 4 sts, k4.
Repeat the last 2 rows 7 times more. Decrease in the next row thus: k4, *k2 tog, k2, rep from * until 3 sts remain, k3 (95 sts).
Purl back and make the ribbon holes as follows:
1st row: k2, *m1, k2 tog, repeat from * to last st, k1.
2nd row: k4, p to last 4 sts, k4.
3rd row: Knit.
4th row: k4, p to last 4 sts, k4.
Make the yoke as follows:
On the first 26 sts proceed as follows (it is wise to mark the end of these sts on your needle).

1st row (right side facing): k4, *k2 tog, k1, m1, k2 tog, k1, m1, k1. Repeat from * to last st, k1.

2nd row: *k2 tog, k1, m1, k2 tog, k1, m1, k1. Repeat from * to last 5 sts, k5.

Repeat these last 2 rows 7 times more. Shape neck by casting off 11 sts. (Because you have to start the pattern row with a k2 tog, I find it easier to k2 tog on the 11th st, then cast off as before; this gives a k2 tog st on the needle and you can finish the row from there.) Work 6 rows on remaining 15 sts for shoulder and cast off.

Back of yoke:

Work the next 43 sts thus:

1st row: *k2 tog, k1, m1, k2 tog, k1, m1, k1. Repeat from * to last st, k1.

Repeat this row until yoke is same length as front yoke. Cast off.

On the remaining 26 sts work the left front yoke as follows:

1st row: *k2 tog, k1, m1, k2 tog, k1, m1, k1. Repeat from * to last 5 sts, k5.

2nd row: k4, *k2 tog, k1, m1, k2 tog, k1, m1, k1. Repeat from * to last st, k1.

Repeat these two rows until work measures the same as right side to neck, cast off 11 sts, and work shoulder to correspond.

Sleeve (both alike)

Cast on 22 sts, and knit three rows.

4th row: Inc thus: k1, k1 twice into each st to end of row (43 sts).

Work 10 rows in stocking st, inc 1 st at each end of 10th row (45 sts).

11th row: Purl.

12th row: Purl.

Work one row knit and 1 row purl, and work pattern as, follows:

1st row: k2, *k2 tog, m1, k1, m1, sl 1, k1, psso, k1. Repeat from * to last st, k1.

2nd row: Purl.

3rd row: k1, k2 tog, *m1, k3, m1, sl 1, k2 tog, psso. Repeat from * to last 6 sts, m1, k3, m1, sl 1, k1, psso, k1.

4th row: Purl.

Repeat these 4 rows once.

9th row: Knit.

10th row: Purl.

11th row: Purl.

12th row: Purl.

13th row: Knit.

14th row: Purl.

Repeat the last 2 rows 3 times more and cast off.

To make up matinee jacket

** Sew up shoulder, side and sleeve seams, and then work neck as follows. With right side of work facing, pick up 82 sts.

Work in ribbon of k1, p1, for two rows, then work ribbon hole row as follows:

Rib 2, *m1, k2 tog, repeat from there to 2 sts, k2.

Rib the next two rows. Cast off. ** Thread ribbon through holes and tie at neck.

Dress

Front

Cast on 83 sts and work the lace edging as follows:

1st row: k2, m1, k3, *sl 1, k2 tog, psso, k3, m1, k1, M1, k3. Repeat from * to last 8 sts, sl 1, k2 tog, psso, k3, m1, k2.

2nd and alternate rows: Purl.

3rd row: *k3, m1, k2, sl 1, k2 tog, psso, k2, m1. Repeat from * to last 3 sts, k3.

5th row: k1, k2 tog, m1,k1, m1, k1, *sl 1, k2 tog, psso k1, m1, k1, m1, sl 1, k2 tog, psso, m1, k1, m1, k1. Repeat from * to last 8 sts, sl 1, k2 tog, psso, k1, m1, k1, m1, k2 tog, k1.

7th row: k1, m1, k1, m1, sl 1, k2 tog, psso, m1, *sl 1, k2 k1 tog, psso, m1, k1, m1, k1, sl 1, k2 tog, psso, k1, m1, k1, m1. Repeat from * to last 8 sts, sl 1, k2 tog, psso, m1, sl 1, k2 tog, psso, m1, k1, m1, k1.

8th row: *p8, p2 tog, rep from * to last 3 sts, p3 (75 sts).

Work 'insertion' pattern as follows:

1st row: Knit.

2nd row: Purl.

Repeat 2nd row twice more.

Repeat 1 st and 2nd rows once more.

7th row: k2, *k2 tog, m1, k1, m1, sl 1, k1, psso, k1. Repeat from * to last st, k1.

8th row: Purl.

9th row: k1, k2 tog, *m1, k3, m1, sl 1, k2 tog, psso. Repeat from * to last 6 sts, m1, k3, m1, sl 1, k1, psso, k1.

10th row: Purl.

Repeat 7th to 10th rows once.

These 14 rows make the pattern.

Repeat these 14 rows three times more, and then repeat rows 1 to 6, decreasing in the 6th row thus: *p2 tog (3 times), p1, repeat from * to last 5 sts, p2 tog (twice), p1 (45 sts).

Make the ribbon holes thus:

1st row: k2, *m1, k2 tog, repeat from * to last st, k1.

2nd row: Purl.

Knit 2 rows, and then purl 2 rows.

Work yoke as follows:

1st row: *k2 tog, k1, m1, k2 tog, k1, m1, k1. Repeat from * to last st, k1.

Repeat this row 3 times more.

Knit 2 rows, purl 2 rows.

Repeat these 8 rows once.

Shape neck and shoulders thus:

Repeat the last 8 rows on the first 15 sts, and cast off.

Shape shoulders and neck thus:

1st row: *k2 tog, k1, m1, k2 tog, k1, m1, k1, rep from * once, k1 (15 sts). Place the last 28 sts on a spare needle. Continue on the 15 sts as follows:

2nd row: Purl.

Knit 2 rows.

Purl 2 rows. Cast off.

Rejoin wool at neck edge, cast off 13 sts loosely for neck and work the remaining 15 sts in pattern to correspond with the other shoulder. Cast off.

To make up dress see instructions for Matinee Jacket ** to **

Back

Work another piece the same as the front.

Sleeve (both alike)

Cast on 43 sts and work 8 rows of lace edging (as given for the first 8 rows of dress). Knit 1 row.

Next row (ribbon holes): p2, *m1, p2 tog, repeat from * to end of row (43 sts).

1st row: Knit.

2nd row: Purl.

3rd row: Purl.

4th row: Purl, inc 1 st at each end of needle (45 sts).

5th row: k2, *k2 tog, m1, k1, m1, sl 1, k1, psso, k1. Repeat from * to last st, k1.

6th row: Purl.

7th row: k1, k2 tog, *m1, k3, m1, sl 1, k2 tog, psso. Repeat from * to last 6 sts, m1, k3, m1, sl 1, psso, k1.

8th row: Purl.

Repeat rows 5 to 8 once.

13th row: Knit.

14th row: Purl.

15th row: Purl.

Cast off.

Bonnet

Cast on 10 sts.

1st row: *k1, k twice into next st, repeat from *

2nd and alternate rows: Knit.

3rd row: *k2, k twice into next st, repeat from *

5th row: *k3, k twice into next st, repeat from *

7th row: *k4, k twice into next st, repeat from *

9th row: *k5, k twice into next st, repeat from *

11th row: *k6, k twice into next st, repeat from *

13th row: *k7, k twice into next st, repeat from (45 sts).

14th row: Knit.

15th row: k2, p to last 2 sts, k2.

Repeat last 2 rows once.

18th row: k2, p to last 2 sts, k2 (right side).

19th row: k2, p to last 2 sts, k2.

20th row: Knit.

21st row: k2, p to last 2 sts, k2.

22nd row: k4, *k2 tog, m1, k1, m1, sl 1, k1, psso, k1, repeat from * to last 3 sts, k3.

23rd row: k2, p to last 2 sts, k2.

24th row: k3, k2 tog, *m1, k3, m1, sl 1, k2 tog, psso. Repeat from * to last 8 sts, m1, k3, m1, sl 1, k1, psso, k3.

25th row: k2, p to last 2 sts, k2.

Repeat 22nd to 25th rows once.

30th row: Knit.

31st, 32nd, 33rd rows: k2, p to last 2 sts, k2.

34th row: Knit.

35th row: k2, p to last 2 sts, k2.

Repeat last 2 rows 3 times more and leave on needle for the time being. Cast on 43 sts, and work the 8 rows of lace edging as given for dress once. Place this needle in front of needle with bonnet sts and join work together by knitting 1 st from each needle tog all along the row. Cast off.

Panties

Cast on 38 sts and work in k1, pt rib for 3 rows.

Ribbon holes thus:

1st row: k1, *m1, k2 tog, repeat from * to last st, k1.

Work 2 more rows of k1, p1.

Work 6 rows in st st, increasing 1 st in the last row (39 sts).

Now work the insertion pattern as follows:

***1st row:* Knit.

2nd row: Purl.

3rd and 4th rows: Purl.

5th row: Knit.

6th row: Purl*

7th row: k2, *k2 tog, m1, k1, m1, sl 1, k1, psso, k1, rep from * to last st, k1.

8th row: Purl.

9th row: k1, k2 tog, *m1, k3, m1, sl 1, k2 tog, psso, rep. from * to last 6 sts, m1, k3, m1, sl 1, k1, psso, k1.

10th row: Purl.

11th row: Repeat 7th row.

12th row: Purl.

13th row: Repeat 9th row.

14th row: Purl**

Repeat 1st to 6th row ** to *.

Shape by k2 tog at each end of the needle in the next 4 rows.

Cast off 3 sts at beginning of next 4 rows.

Then k2 tog at both ends of the needle for 3 rows. Cast off.

Make other half exactly the same.

Sew up panties, trim leg with shell edging to match armhole of vest. Thread ribbon at waist.

Vest

Cast on 33 sts and work in k1, p1 rib for 2 rows. Work 30 rows of st st.

Work the 14 rows of insertion pattern as given in the panties from ** to **.

To shape top of vest:

Cast off 5 sts (for armhole), slip 4 sts onto a safety pin.

Cast off 15 sts (neck), slip next 4 sts onto safety pin. Cast off remaining 5 sts.

Rejoin wool to the first 4 sts.

Work 16 rows in garter st for shoulder strap. Cast off.

Rejoin wool to the other 4 sts, work 16 rows in garter st. Cast off.

Make another piece exactly the same for the back.

Sew up seams of vest and work ribbon beading around neck. Around armholes work thus: 2 tr into edge, miss 2 sts, 1 dc into next st and repeat all around. (US readers: 2 dc into edge, miss 2 sts, 1 sc into next st and repeat all around.)

Bootees

Cast on 21 sts and knit one row. Shape as follows:

1st row: k1, k twice into next st, k3, k twice into next st, k1, k twice into next st, k7, k twice into next st, k1.

2nd and alternate rows: Knit.

3rd row: k1, k twice into next st, k9, k twice into next st, k1, k twice into next st, k9, k twice into next st, k1.

5th row: k1, k twice into next st, k11, k twice into next st, k1, k twice into next st, k11, k twice into next st, k1.

Shape instep thus: k18, k2 tog, *turn, k5, k2 tog. Repeat from * until you have 27 sts.

Work all the sts on one needle and work the two rows of ribbon holes as given for frock.

Knit 1 row, purl 3 rows, knit 1 row, purl 1 row, and work 8 fancy pattern rows, then knit 1 row, purl 2 rows.

Purl 1 row, at the same time reducing sts to 24.

Work two rows of k1, p1 rib and cast off loosely ribwise.

SAPPHIRE *Illustrated on page 50*

This set, worked in 2-ply wool, is ideally suited to any 46 cm (18") celluloid baby doll, bisque-headed baby or composition baby doll of the 1930s. The set consists of dress, bonnet, pilchers and shoettes and has been adapted from instructions first printed in the Australian Home Journal *in December 1935.*

Materials

50 g (2 oz) 2-ply wool (I used Bendigo, but any good 2-ply wool can be used)
Pair 3.75 mm (9) (US 5) knitting needles
2 m (2¼ yds) baby ribbon
2 buttons
Fine crochet hook

Measurements

Dress Length from shoulder to hem	28 cm (11")	
Width at underarm	36 cm (14")	
Sleeve seam	7 cm (3")	
Bonnet Face edge	23 cm (9")	
Depth (front to back)	13 cm (5")	
Pilchers Waist	30.5 cm (12")	
Waist to crutch	15 cm (6")	
Leg seam	10 cm (4")	
Shoettes Length of foot	6.5 cm (2½")	

Tension

7 sts to 2.5 cm (1") over st st; 9 rows to 2.5 cm (1") over st st.

Dress

Front

Commence at lower edge and cast on 83 sts. Knit one row into back of cast-on sts, then commence pattern as follows:
1st row: k2, m1, k3, *sl 1, k2 tog, psso, k3, m1, k1, m1, k3. Repeat from * to last 8 sts, sl 1, k2 tog, psso, k3, m1, k2.
2nd row: k1, p to last st, k1.
3rd row: *k3, m1, k2, sl 1, k2 tog, psso, k2, m1. Repeat from * to last 3 sts, k3.
4th row: Repeat 2nd row.
5th row: k1, k2 tog, m1, k1, m1, k1, *sl 1, k2 tog, psso, k1, m1, k1, m1, sl 1, k2 tog, psso, m1, k1, m1, k1. Repeat from * to last 8 sts, sl 1, k2 tog, psso, k1, m1, k1, m1, k2 tog, k1.
6th row: Repeat 2nd row.
7th row: k1, m1, k1, m1, sl 1, k2 tog, psso, m1, *sl 1, k2

tog, psso, m1, k1, m1, k1, sl 1, k2 tog, psso, k1, m1, k1, m1. Repeat from * to last 8 sts, sl 1, k2 tog, psso, m1, sl 1, k2 tog, psso, m1, k1, m1, k1.
8th row: Repeat 2nd row.
These 8 rows complete the pattern. Repeat the pattern 8 times more.
Knit 1 row, dec the number of stitches thus: *k1, k2 tog, repeat from * to last st, k1 (56 sts).
Knit 1 row.
Make the ribbon holes as follows:
1st row: k1, *wool over needle twice, k2 tog. Repeat from * to last st, k1.
2nd row: k1, *then knit the stitch and purl the loop (letting both loops off the needle). Repeat from * to last st, k1.
The pattern for yoke is worked thus:
1st row: Knit.
2nd row: Purl.
3rd row: k1, *k2 tog, repeat from * to last st, k1.
4th row: k1, *then pick up and knit the loop before the next st, k1. Repeat from * to last st, k1 (56 sts).
Cast off 4 sts at beginning of next 2 rows. Taking care to keep pattern correct, continue without decreasing until yoke is 7.5 cm (3") deep.
Work 14 sts in pattern, cast off 20 sts, work remaining 14 sts in pattern. Continue on these 14 sts for 12 mm (½"). Cast off. Work other shoulder the same.
The back of the dress is made exactly the same.

Sleeve (two alike)

Cast on 30 sts and knit 3 rows, then knit 1 row and increase in next row.
K1, *k1, inc in next st, repeat from * to end of row (43 sts).
Repeat the 8 pattern rows 4 times on these 43 sts. Cast off loosely.
Make another sleeve in exactly the same manner.

To make up

Do not press. Sew up underarm, sleeve and right shoulder seam. Sew in sleeves, placing seam to seam. Fasten shoulder with the buttons and thread ribbon through holes at waist. (As this is a very lacy pattern, I suggest you make a satin slip to go under the dress. The slip could be off white, pale pink or blue.)

Bonnet

Cast on 67 sts and knit 1 row. Proceed as follows:

1st row: k4, m1, k3, *sl 1, k2 tog, psso, k3, m1, k1, m1, k3. Repeat from * to last 10 sts, sl 1, k2 tog, psso, k3, m1, k4.

2nd row: k3, p to last 3 sts, k3.

3rd row: k2, *k3, m1, k2, sl 1, k2 tog, psso, k2, m1. Repeat from * to last 5 sts, k5.

4th row: Repeat 2nd row.

5th row: k3, k2 tog, m1, k1, m1, k1, *sl 1, k2 tog, psso, k1, m1, k1, m1, sl 1, k2 tog, psso, m1, k1, m1, k1. Repeat from * to last 10 sts, sl 1, k2 tog, psso, k1, m1, k1, m1, k2 tog, k3.

6th row: Repeat 2nd row.

7th row: k3, m1, k1, m1, sl 1, k2 tog, psso, m1, *sl 1, k2 tog, psso, m1, k1, m1, k1, sl 1, k2 tog, psso, k1, m1, k1, m1. Repeat from * to last 10 sts, sl 1, k2 tog, psso, m1, sl 1, k2 tog, psso, m1, k1, m1, k3.

8th row: Repeat row 2.

Repeat these 8 rows 5 times more, then knit 2 rows, dec to 60 sts in last row.

Shape crown thus:

1st row: *k8, k2 tog, repeat from * to end of row.

2nd and alternate rows: Knit.

3rd row: *k7, k2 tog, repeat from * to end of row.

5th row: *k6, k2 tog, repeat from * to end of row.

7th row: *k5, k2 tog, repeat from * to end of row.

9th row: *k4, k2 tog, repeat from * to end of row.

11th row: *k3, k2 tog, repeat from * to end of row.

13th row: *k2, k2 tog, repeat from * to end of row.

15th row: *k1, k2 tog, repeat from * to end of row.

Run a darning needle through the remaining stitches, draw into a small circle and sew crown down to last row of pattern.

Attach rosettes and ribbon ties.

Pilchers

Cast on 23 sts and knit 1 row into back of cast-on sts. Increase 1 st at both ends of the needle every alternate row until you have 43 sts.

Repeat the 8 pattern rows 4 times, dec one st in the last row to give 42 sts for ribbing.

Work in rib of k2, p2 for 12 mm (½"), then make a row of ribbon holes as given for frock. Continue in the ribbing for 12 mm (½") and cast off loosely from the wrong side. Make another half exactly the same. Sew up side and under crutch, thread ribbon at the waist and crochet edging around the legs as given below for the shoettes.

Shoettes

Cast on 24 sts and knit 1 row.

2nd row: k11, knit twice into next 2 sts, k11.

3rd row: Knit.

4th row: k11, knit twice into next 4 sts, k11.

5th row: Knit.

6th row: k13, knit twice into next 4 sts, k13.

Knit 3 rows.

10th row: k13, *k7, k2 tog, turn*, repeat from * to * until you have 27 sts.

Knit all the stitches on to one needle.

Make a row of ribbon holes and cast off loosely.

Make another shoette the same way.

To make up

Sew up shoe, and crochet an edging around the top: *2 ch, 2 tr into same stitch, 1 dc, 6 mm along. Repeat from *. (US readers: *2 ch, 2 dc into same stitch, 1 sc, ¼" along, repeat from *)

Thread with ribbon.

TOPAZ *Illustrated on page 39*

A fascinating and irresistible baby doll's layette, adapted from a 1937 pattern, for a 23–25 cm (9"–10") baby doll which will delight the collector as well as the small daughter of the house. Included in the set are vest, panties, princess slip and a lacy frock, all knitted in white, topped off by a bonnet and long coat in a delicate baby shade.

Like all the other patterns in this book, this delightful set can be made to fit a larger doll simply by using a thicker ply wool and larger needles.

Materials

50 g (2 oz) 3-ply baby wool in white
50 g (2 oz) 3-ply baby wool in pink or another delicate colour
(*or* 100 g (4 oz) baby wool if set is knitted in one colour)
Pair 2.75 mm (12) (US 2) knitting needles
Fine crochet hook
2 m (2¼ yds) narrow baby ribbon

Measurements

Coat Shoulder to hem	17.5 cm (7")
Width around underarm	20 cm (8")
Width around hem	43 cm (17")
Length of sleeve (without cuff)	7 cm (2¾")
Depth of collar	5 cm (2")
Bonnet Face edge	13 cm (5")
To start of turnback brim	6 cm (2½")
Dress Shoulder to hem	14.5 cm (5¾")
Around waist	18 cm (7")
Sleeve seam	3 cm (1¼")
Slip Shoulder to hem	13.5 cm (5¼")
Around waist	19 cm (7½")
Vest Shoulder to hem	8 cm (3¼")
Around underarm	14 cm (5½")
Panties Waist to crutch	7.5 cm (3")
Around waist	16.5 cm (6½")
Leg seam	4.5 cm (1¾")

Tension

8 sts to 2.5 cm (1") over st st; 13 rows to 2.5 cm (1") over st st.

Vest

Cast on 26 sts and work 4 rows of single rib and 20 rows of st st.
To shape the armholes:
Cast off 3 sts at the beginning of the next 2 rows (20 sts).

Work 4 rows in st st to the neckline.
Next row: k7, slip the remaining 13 sts onto a large safety pin.
Work 8 rows on the first 7 sts and cast off.
Rejoin wool at neck edge and cast off 6 sts.
On the remaining 7 sts, work 9 rows and cast off.
Knit a second piece exactly the same and join the two pieces together at the shoulders.

Neck edge:
Working loosely so that the vest will fit easily over the doll's head:
1st row: 1 dc into each st. Slip st into the first dc.
2nd row: 4 ch, miss 1 dc along the row, *1 dc in the next st, 1 ch, miss 1 dc, 1 tr in the next st and repeat from * all around. Slip st into 2nd ch.
3rd row: 2 dc in each space all around, slip st into the first st. Fasten off. (US readers: refer to page 11 for the American equivalents of these crochet terms.)

Panties

Begin at the waistline and cast on 28 sts.
Work 2 rows in single rib.
Next row: k1, *m1, k2 tog, repeat from * until 1 st remains, k1.
Work 3 more rows in single rib.
1st row: k1, inc in next st, knit to the last 2 sts, inc in next st, k1.
2nd row: Purl.
Repeat these 2 rows until there are 40 sts on the needle.
Purl 1 row.
Leg shaping:
Cast off 2 sts at the beginning of the next 14 rows (12 sts).
Next row: k2 tog at each end of row.
Purl 1 row.
Repeat the last 2 rows once (8 sts). Cast off.
Work a second piece to match.
Join up the side seams and under the crutch.

Work a little crochet edging round each leg as follows:
1 dc in the first st, *3 ch, miss 1 dc, 1 dc in the next st, and repeat from * all around, sl st into the first st, and fasten off. (See page 11 for equivalent American terms.)

Princess slip

Cast on 37 sts.
1st row: Knit.
2nd row: Purl.
3rd row: k1, *m1, k2 tog, repeat from * to end of row.
4th row: As 3rd row.
Repeat the last 4 rows once.
Work 34 rows in st st to the armholes, then repeat 3rd row.
Next row: Purl.
To shape the armholes:
Cast off 4 sts at the beginning of the next 2 rows, then cast off 2 sts at the beginning of the following 4 rows (21 sts).
Work 4 rows in st st (neckline).
First shoulder:
Knit 7 and leave the remaining 14 sts on a spare needle or large safety pin.
Work 8 rows in st st on these 7 sts. Cast off.
Rejoin wool to neck edge, cast off 7 sts, and work 9 rows on the remaining 7 sts. Cast off.
Work a second piece exactly the same.

To make up
Join the two pieces together at the shoulders and work a tiny crochet edging around the neck and armholes as for the edge of the panties. Press the pieces on the wrong side. Sew up side seams and press finished garment. Thread ribbon through the holes at the waist.

Dress

Beginning at the lower edge of the back, cast on 52 sts. Knit 1 row into the back of the sts to make a neat edge, then work the pattern as follows:
1st row: Knit.
2nd row: Purl.
3rd row: *k1, m1, k2 tog, rep from * until 1 st remains, k1.
4th row: As 3rd row.
Repeat these 4 rows 12 times more.
Next row: k2 tog all along the row (26 sts).
Next row: Purl.
To shape the armholes:
Cast off 3 sts at beg of each of the next 2 rows (20 sts).
Work 12 rows in st st to the neckline.
Work 7 sts and leave remaining 13 sts on spare needle.
On these 7 sts work 6 rows in st st and cast off.

Rejoin wool to neck edge, cast off 6 sts, and work 7 rows in st st on remaining 7 sts. Cast off.
Work a second piece for the front. Join the two pieces together, at the outside edge only of the shoulder seams.

Sleeves
With the wrong side of the dress facing, pick up and purl 52 sts around the armhole.
Repeat the 4 rows of the pattern 3 times.
Next row: k2 tog all along the row.
Work 2 rows in st st and cast off.
Work a second sleeve the same way.
Work a small buttonhole on one side of each shoulder, and sew a button on the other.

To make up
Work a tiny edging around the front and back of the neck like the edging on the panties. Press the dress on the wrong side. Sew up the side seams.

Coat

Back
Beginning at the lower edge of the back, cast on 52 sts and work 58 rows in spaced moss st as follows:
1st row: *k1, p1, repeat from * along row.
2nd row: Purl.
3rd row: *p1, k1, repeat from * along row.
4th row: Purl.
After the 58 rows, work 3 rows in single rib, k1, p1.
Decrease sts for yoke:
Next row: k1, *p2 tog, repeat from * until 1 st remains, k1 (27 sts).
Work 4 rows in pattern to the armholes ***
To shape the armholes:
Cast off 3 sts at beginning of each next 2 rows (21 sts).
Work 12 rows on these sts to the back neckline.
To form the shoulder:
Continuing in patt, work 6 rows on the first 6 sts. Cast off.
Rejoin wool to neck edge, cast off 9 sts and work 6 rows in pattern on the remaining 6 sts and cast off.

Right front
Cast on 42 sts, and work in pattern as per back of coat to the armhole *** (22 sts).
Work 1 row, finishing at the armhole end (do not work this row on the left front).
Next row (wrong side): Cast off 4 sts, and work in pattern to the front edge.
Next row: Work in pattern to armhole.
Next row: Work 2 tog, and then work in pattern to end.
Work 8 rows in pattern to the neckline.

To shape the neck:
Cast off 11 sts and work to the end of the row (6 sts). Work 6 rows more on these 6 sts. Cast off.

Left front
Work to match the right front, but reverse the shaping by casting off the armhole sts on the right side (do not work the extra row to the armhole).
Cast off the neck sts at the beginning of a wrong side row, then work as for the right front.

Sleeves
Cast on 26 sts for the top of the sleeve and, working in the same pattern as the back, work 1 row.
Continuing in pattern cast on 2 sts at beginning of the next 4 rows, and inc 1 st at beginning of the next 2 rows (36 sts). Dec 1 st at both ends of the 4th row and every following 4th row until 22 sts remain.
Work 3 rows.

Cuff
Next row (right side): Knit, increasing 1 st at each end of row (24 sts).
Next row (wrong side): Work the first row of the pattern (so when the cuff is turned over, the right side of the pattern will be uppermost).
Work 8 rows in pattern and cast off.
Work a second sleeve the same.

Cape collar
Beginning at the lower edge, cast on 108 sts and work 1st row of coat back pattern.
Next row (wrong side): (*p12*, p2 tog) 3 times, p24, (p2 tog, *p12*) 3 times.
3rd row: Work as 3rd row of coat pattern.
4th row (wrong side): (*p11*, p2 tog) 3 times, p24, (p2 tog, *p11*) 3 times.
5th row: Work as 3rd row.
6th row (wrong side): (*p10*, p2 tog) 3 times, p 24, (p2 tog, *p10*) 3 times.
Repeat the last 2 rows, decreasing by 1 st the number of p sts in the brackets in every wrong side row (as set between * *), until number of stitches has been reduced to 36 sts overall on needle.
Work 2 rows in pattern and cast off.

To make up
Sew the shoulder seams and sew the sleeves into the armholes. Sew the cape in position around the neck edge of the coat, leaving about 2 cm (¾") free on each side of the front edge to form an overlap. Sew up the side seams. With a suitable size crochet hook and angora wool, work 1 dc (US sc) around the outside edge of the collar, missing a st here and there to keep the work flat. Work a similar edge up the right front. Work 2 button loops on the right front (one at the neck and another at the high waistline). If the coat is made as a double-breasted coat, sew two extra buttons in place to match.

Bonnet

Begin at the centre back by casting on 12 sts, and work the first row in pattern.
2nd row: (p1, inc by purling in the back and front of the next st) 6 times.
Repeat these 2 rows until you have 36 sts; remembering that after each repetition of the 2nd row there will be 1 more st between the increases.
Work 24 rows in pattern.
Work 1 row plain on the right side of work.
Next row (wrong side): Work the first row of the pattern (this will reverse the work, and when the brim is turned back it will be on the outside of the bonnet).
Work 8 rows in pattern.
With angora wool work 1 dc (US sc) into each knitted st, slipping it off the knitting needle as the dc is worked. Work a second row of dc (US sc) and fasten off. Thread a darning needle, run it through the cast-on sts and draw into a little circle, and then sew along the seam for about 2.5 cm (1") at the back of the bonnet. Finish off with ribbon ties.

Bootees

With 2 mm (14) (US 0) needles and main colour, cast on 22 sts.
Work two rows in k1, p1 rib (beginning each row with a k1).
1st row: *p1, k1, repeat from * to end of row.
2nd row: Purl.
3rd row: *k1, p1, repeat from * to end of row.
4th row: Purl.
Repeat 1st and 2nd rows.
Ribbon hole row: k1, *(m1, k2 tog), repeat from * to end of row.
Purl one row.
Divide the sts for the instep as follows:
Knit 14, turn, p6, (leaving 8 sts unworked at each side).
Work 6 rows in st st on the centre 6 sts.
Next row: Knit the 6 instep sts, pick up and knit 6 sts along side of instep, then k8 sts.
Next row: Purl 20 sts, pick up 6 sts along side of instep, and purl to end.
Work 5 rows in st st. Cast off.
Work another bootee the same. Join the underfoot and side seams. Thread ribbon through slots at ankles.

TOURMALINE *Illustrated on page 51*

This lovely baby doll layette consists of bonnet, dress, coat, vest, panties and bootees. Worked in 2-ply wool in a version of the traditional pattern known as 'Feather and Fan' it is within the capability of all knitters. The main pieces have an unusual edge of mohair or angora. The outfit, adapted from a 1930s/1940s Xmas Doll Set (printed by John Sands for the Australian Home Journal), fits a 30 cm (12") doll and because of the type of pattern is equally at home on a doll of any age. If done in 3-ply wool and 4 mm (8) (US 6) needles, the pattern should fit a 45 cm (18") doll.

Materials

100 g (4 oz) 2-ply wool in main colour (I used Bendigo 2-ply)

25 g (1 oz) 2-ply wool in white (for undies)

Small ball of white mohair or angora wool (for the trim)

Pair 3.5 mm (10) (US 4) needles

Pair 2 mm (14) (US 0) needles for bootees

5 m (5½ yds) ribbon to match main colour

1 m (1 yd) white ribbon for undies

3 small buttons (1 for the dress, 2 for the vest)

Small crochet hook (for trim)

Measurements

Dress Shoulder to hem	21.5 cm	(8½")
Waist measurement	33 cm	(13")
Sleeve seam	6.5 cm	(2½")
Jacket Shoulder to hem	14 cm	(5½")
Waist measurement	33 cm	(13")
Width around hem	60 cm	(23½")
Sleeve seam	10 cm	(4")
Bonnet Face edge	20 cm	(8")
Front to back	9 cm	(3½")
Vest Shoulder to hem	13.5 cm	(5¼")
Underarm measurement	25 cm	(10")
Neck to hem	10 cm	(4")
Panties Waist measurement	28 cm	(11")
Waist to crutch	11.5 cm	(4½")
Side seam	8 cm	(3¼")
Bootees Length of foot	5 cm	(2")

Tension

7 sts to 2.5 cm (1") over st st; 9 rows to 2.5 cm (1") over st st.

Dress

With 3.5 mm (10) (US 4) needles and white mohair (or angora) wool, cast on 84 sts. Break off wool and join in main colour.

Next row: Knit into back of cast-on stitches.

Knit 1 row.

1st row: (k2 tog) twice, *(m1, k1) four times, (k2 tog) four times. Repeat from * to last four stitches, (k2 tog) twice.

2nd row: Knit.

3nd row: Knit.

4th row: Purl ** These four rows form the pattern.

Repeat pattern 14 times.

Next row: k1, *k2 tog, repeat from * to last st, k1.

Next row: Purl.

Ribbon holes: k1, *m1, k2 tog, repeat from * to end of row.

Next row: Purl.

Work 6 rows in moss stitch.

Cast on 14 sts at beg of the next two rows for sleeves, and work 12 rows in moss st.

Next row: Work 25 sts in moss st, cast off 20 sts, work remaining 25 sts in moss st.

Work 11 rows of moss st on these last 25 sts.

Next row: Cast on 10 sts at the neck edge and work 11 rows in moss st.

Cast off 14 sts (for sleeve) and work 5 rows in moss st. Cast off.

Rejoin wool to other half and work the other shoulder and back of bodice to match.

Back

Work the same number of patterns as the front (15 patterns).

Next row: k1, *k2 tog, rep from * to last st, k1.

Next row: Purl.

Work the ribbon hole row.

Next row: Knit. Cast off.

To make up

Sew back of skirt to back bodice. Sew up side seams.

Work a row of dc around neck, and make ribbon holes as follows: *1 tr, 2 ch, miss 2 sts, repeat from * to end. If your doll has a large head, the neck can be finished by working a loose shell edge. (US readers: refer to page 11 for American crochet equivalents.)

Crochet a small shell pattern around sleeves to finish off. Thread ribbon at waist and neck if desired.

Jacket

Back

Using 3.5 mm (10) (US 4) needles and white mohair (or angora) wool, cast on 72 sts. Break off, and join in main colour.

With main colour knit into back of cast-on stitches.

Knit 1 row.

Work 8 patterns as given for front of frock.

Row 33: Dec for bodice by working 2 tog all along the row.

Next row: Purl.

Work ribbon holes: k1, *(m1, k2 tog), rep from * to last st, k1.

Next row: Purl.

Work 16 rows in st.

Shoulders

Knit 15, turn p to end.

Next row: Continue in st st, k2 tog at end of row (neck edge), and next 2 alt rows.

Work 2 rows in st st. Cast off.

Rejoin wool at neck edge, cast off 6 sts and work remaining 15 sts to match other shoulder.

Front (two the same)

Cast on 54 sts with white mohair (or angora) wool, break off and join in main colour.

Knit into back of cast-on sts.

Knit 1 row.

1st row: (k2 tog) twice, *(m1, k1) four times, (k2 tog) four times. Rep from * to last 10 sts, then k2 tog twice, k6.

2nd row: Knit.

3rd row: k6, p to end of row.

Repeat the last 4 rows 7 times (8 patterns).

Continue as from row 33 of the back, but keeping the k6 border until shoulder has been reached.

Shape shoulder:

Knit 1 row.

Next row: Cast off till you have 15 sts left (including the one on needle). Work to end of row. Continue working in st st, shaping neck edge by working 2 sts tog at neck edge in next, and following 2 alt rows.

Work 3 rows in st st. Cast off.

Work other front to correspond, making sure that you work the 6 st border at the beginning of the 1st row, and end of

the 4th row, of pattern, and that you cast off and dec from the border (or neck) edge.

Sleeves (two alike)

Cast on 28 sts with white mohair (or angora) wool, break off and join in main colour.

Next row: Knit into back of cast-on sts.

Knit 1 row.

Ribbon holes: k1, *(m1, k2 tog), rep from * to last st, k1.

Work 3 rows st st, commencing with a purl row and increasing 8 sts evenly on last purl row (36 sts).

Repeat pattern as given for back of coat, 10 times. Cast off.

Work another sleeve to match.

To make up

Sew shoulders together, fronts to back. Fold sleeve in half and mark top. Sew this to shoulder seam, and gently sew sleeve into position, down each side, back and front. Sew up side seams.

Make ribbon holes around neck as follows:

1st row: dc, turn.

2nd row: *1 tr, 2 ch, miss 2 sts and rep from * to end. Finish off.

Thread ribbon at neck, waist and sleeves.

(US readers: refer to page 11 for equivalent American terms.)

Bonnet

With 3.5 mm (10) (US 4) needles and white mohair (or angora) wool, cast on 60 sts, break off and join in main colour.

Repeat the pattern as given for front of frock 8 times.

Shape crown as follows:

1st row: *k8, k2 tog, repeat from * to end of row.

2nd and alternate rows: Knit.

3rd row: *k7, k2 tog, rep from * to end of row.

5th row: *k6, k2 tog, rep from * to end of row.

7th row: *k5, k2 tog, rep from * to end of row.

9th row: *k4, k2 tog, rep from * to end of row.

11th row: *k3, k2 tog, rep from * to end of row.

13th row: *k2, k2 tog, rep from * to end of row.

15th row: *k1, k2 tog, rep from * to end of row. Break off, leaving a long thread to thread into a darning needle.

Run darning needle through the remaining sts, draw up, and fasten off securely. Sew back of bonnet to beg of crown.

Crochet a row of ribbon holes around bottom edge of bonnet if desired, as follows:

1st row: dc around back of bonnet, commencing at front, turn.

2nd row: *1 tr, 2 ch, rep from * around to other side. Attach ribbon to either side, thread through ribbon holes and tie at the nape of the neck in a bow.

Or, make a rosette from ribbon, and attach to one side of bonnet, leaving a long enough piece to tie. Make a similar rosette and tie for other side.

Panties (worked in one piece)

Using white 2-ply wool, cast on 48 sts.
Knit in ribbing of k2, p2 for 4 rows.
Next row: k1, *m1, k2 tog, rep from * to last st, k1.
Work 4 more rows of rib.
Repeat pattern as given for front of frock 6 times.
Work in moss st, dec 1 st at each end of the needle in every row until 16 sts remain.
Work 8 rows in moss st without dec, then inc 1 st at each end of the needle in every row until there are 48 sts.
Work 6 patterns, then 4 rows of rib, 1 row of ribbon holes, and 4 more rows of rib. Cast off.

Vest

Using white 2-ply wool cast on 36 sts. Knit into the back of cast-on sts.
Repeat pattern as given for front of frock 10 times.
Next row: (k2 tog) twice, *(m1, k1) four times, (k2 tog) four times. Repeat from * to the last 4 sts, k2 tog twice.
Work 8 rows in moss st.

Next row: Work 11 moss st, turn, and working only on these 11 sts work 9 rows in moss st. Cast off.
Rejoin wool at neck and cast off 14 sts. Work 10 rows of moss st on remaining 11 sts and cast off.
Work another side exactly the same.
Sew up side seams as far as the yoke. Sew right shoulder together. Crochet shell pattern around neck to finish off.
Sew two small buttons on the opposite shoulder.

Bootees

With white mohair (or angora) wool and 3.5 mm (10) (US 4) needles, cast on 24 sts, break off wool, join in main colour.
Knit 2 rows (knitting into the back of the stitches in the 1st knit row).
Work 2 patterns as given for front of frock.
Ribbon slot: k1, *(m1, k2 tog), rep from * to last st, k1.
Purl 1 row.
Divide the sts for instep as follows:
Knit 16, turn, p8, turn.
Work 8 rows in st st on these 8 sts.
Next row: k8, pick up 7 sts along side of instep, knit remaining 8 sts.
Next row: p23, pick up 7 sts along side of instep, purl remaining 8 sts.
Work 6 rows in moss st. Cast off.
Work another bootee the same. Join leg and underfoot seams. Thread ribbon through slots at ankles.

TURQUOISE
Illustrated on page 52

This layette for a 31 cm (12") baby doll has been adapted from a 1938 English Woman's Weekly pattern. It consists of dress, bootees, sleeved vest and pilchers, all worked in white 2-ply, and a jacket and matching bonnet worked in a pretty pastel colour with ribbons to match. The outfit is ideal for either a bisque-headed baby doll or a small celluloid or composition doll, but would look equally at home on a more modern plastic doll with the same measurements.

Materials
50 g (2 oz) Shepherd 2-ply baby wool in white (or Bendigo 2-ply)
25 g (1 oz) Patons 3-ply baby wool in a delicate baby shade
Pair 3.25 mm (10) (US 4) knitting needles
Pair 2.75 mm (12) (US 2) knitting needles
2.5 mm (10) (US C) crochet hook
3 m (3¼ yds) matching baby ribbon
3 small buttons

Measurements
Frock Length	18 cm (7")
Around body	28 cm (11")
Sleeve seam	7.5 cm (3")
Jacket Around body	28 cm (11")
Shoulder to hem	12.5 cm (5")
Bonnet Face edge	18 cm (7")
Back to front	8 cm (3¼")
Vest Length	12.5 cm (5")
Around body	23 cm (9")
Pilchers Around body	23 cm (9")
Waist to crutch	10 cm (4")
Bootees Length of foot	4.5 cm (1¾")

Tension
8 sts to 2.5 cm (1") over st st; 11 rows to 2.5 cm (1") over st st.

Vest

Using white 2-ply wool and 2.75 mm (12) (US 2) needles, cast on 38 sts, and work 6 rows in single rib, working into the back of the sts on the first row to give a neat edge.
Work 38 rows in st st to the armhole. (If you wish you may have fewer rows here to make a shorter garment.)
To shape the armholes:
Continue in st st, decreasing at the beginning of each of the next 9 rows (32 sts).
Work 6 rows straight to the neck.

Neck opening:
Work 4 sts in st st, and slip these sts onto a spare needle. Cast off 24 sts and work 7 rows on the remaining 4 sts.
Join the wool to the neck edge of the 4 sts on the spare needle and work 6 rows. Cast off.
Work a second piece the same way.
Neck band:
Join one shoulder seam, and then pick up 60 sts all around the neck edge.
Work 3 rows in single rib, k1, p1. Cast off loosely so it will go over the doll's head.
Work a small button hole on one edge of the remaining shoulder and sew a small flat button on the other side to fasten.

Sleeves
Cast on 26 sts and work 3 rows in single rib.
Work 16 rows in st st.
Decrease at the beginning of the next 6 rows (20 sts). Cast off.
Work a second sleeve the same.

To make up
First press all pieces following the instructions on page 6. Set sleeves into armholes. Join sleeve and side seams in one long line and give a final light press.

Pilchers

Using white 2-ply wool and 2.75 mm (12) (US 2) needles, cast on 12 sts and work 1 row into the back of the sts to give a neat edge.
Continue in st st, casting on 3 sts at the beginning of each of the next 10 rows (42 sts).
Work 18 rows in st st. (If you want a shorter pair of pants, work fewer rows here.)
Continue in st st, decreasing at both ends of the next row.
Work 7 rows in st st.
Repeat the last 8 rows once more.

Work 4 rows in single rib.

1st slot row: k1, *k2 tog, repeat from * until 1 st remains, k1.

2nd slot row: p1, *pick up 1, k1, repeat from * until 1 st remains, p1.

Work 2 rows in single rib. Cast off.

Work a second piece the same.

To make up

First press both pieces following instructions on page 00. Join the 2 cast-on edges. Pick up 32 sts from around the first leg and knit 3 rows. Cast off.

Work the other leg the same way.

Join both side seams.

Thread baby ribbon through the slots at the waist and tie at the centre front.

Dress

Back

Using white wool and 3.25 mm (10) (US 4) needles, cast on 57 sts.

Knit 2 rows, working into the back of the sts on the first row to give a neat edge.

Work in pattern as follows:

1st row: k1, *k2 tog, m1, k the next st double (by knitting through the loop of the same st on the previous row instead of the loop on the needle, and slip both off the needle together), m1, k2 tog, repeat from * until 1 st remains, k1.

2nd row: Knit.

These 2 rows complete the pattern.

Repeat the 2 pattern rows 24 times more.

Decrease row: k3, *k3, k2 tog, repeat from * until 4 sts remain, k4 (47 sts).

Purl 1 row.

1st slot row: k1, *k2 tog, repeat from * to end.

2nd slot row: *p1, pick up 1, repeat from * until 1 st remains, p1.

Change to 2.75 mm (12) (US 2) needles and work 4 rows in st st.

To shape armholes:

Continue in st st, dec at both ends of the next row and following 3 alt rows (39 sts), ending with a knit row.

Next row: Knit.

Work 4 rows in st st, decreasing at both ends of the next row and following alternate row, beginning with a k row (35 sts).

Work 3 rows straight in st st.

To shape neck:

Next row: p5, slip these sts onto a stitch holder until needed. Cast off 25 sts, and purl the remaining 5 sts.

Work 4 rows in st st on these 5 sts. (Work 7 rows here on front.) Cast off.

Join wool to the neck edge of opposite shoulder sts, and work 4 rows. (Work 6 rows here on front.) Cast off.

Neck edge:

With 2.75 mm (12) (US 2) needles, pick up 35 sts (37 on front) from around the neck edge.

Rib one row. Cast off.

Front

Work exactly the same as for the back, noting the differences given in brackets.

Sleeves

With 2.75 mm (12) (US 2) needles, cast on 24 sts, and work 8 rows in single rib.

Continue in st st, inc 1 st at both ends of the next row and every following 8th row until 3 inc rows have been worked (30 sts).

Work 8 rows straight.

Continue in st st, decreasing at the beginning of each of the next 8 rows. Cast off.

Work a second sleeve the same.

To make up

Press all pieces, following instructions on page 6, on the wrong side of the work. Set sleeves into the armholes. Make a buttonhole loop on each shoulder. Fasten with 2 tiny buttons. Thread ribbon through holes at waist. Work one row of tiny satin sts (in the colour of the coat and bonnet) to form spots on each side of the plain knit rows on the yoke.

Bootees

With 2.75 mm (12) (US 2) needles and white wool, cast on 24 sts, and work 10 rows in single rib.

1st slot row: k1, *k2 tog, repeat from * until 1 st remains, k1.

2nd slot row: k1, *pick up 1, p1, repeat from * until 1 st remains, k1.

Next row: k15, turn (slip remaining 9 sts onto safety pin).

Next row: p6, turn (slip the other remaining 9 sts onto a safety pin).

Work 10 rows in st st on the remaining middle 6 sts.

On same needle pick up 6 sts along one side of middle strip, and then the 9 sts from safety pin on that side.

Knit 1 row, then pick up 6 sts from the other side of the instep, and finally the remaining 9 sts (36 sts).

Knit 6 rows.

Decrease row: k2 tog, k11, k2 tog, k6, k2 tog, k11, k2 tog. Cast off.

Join back of leg and underfoot seam. Thread ribbon through holes at ankle.

Knit another bootee the same.

Coat

With 3.25 mm (10) (US 4) needles and coloured wool, cast on 77 sts.

Knit 3 rows, working into the back of the sts on the first row to give a neat edge.

Work in pattern as follows:

1st row: Knit.

2nd row: k2, *p1, k2, repeat from * to end.

3rd row: Knit.

4th row: k2, *k1, p2, repeat from * until 3 sts remain, k3.

Repeat these 4 rows once, then the 1st and 2nd rows again.

Next row: Knit.

Next row: k3, p2, k1, purl until 6 sts remain, k1, p2, k3.

Next row: Knit.

Next row: k2, p1, k2, purl until 5 sts remain, k2, p1, k2.

Repeat the last 4 rows twice more.

Divide for armholes:

Knit 57 sts and slip the remaining 20 sts onto a spare needle until needed for the left front.

Next row, p37, turn and slip the other 20 sts onto a stitch holder for the right front.

Back

On the remaining 37 sts continue in st st, dec at the beginning of each of the next 12 rows (25 sts).

Continue straight on these sts for 10 rows. Cast off.

Left front

Join wool to shoulder edge of left front and, continuing in pattern (keeping 6 st borders) dec at armhole end of next and following 5 alt rows (14 sts).

Continue straight on these sts for 6 rows.

To shape neck:

Cast off 10 sts at the beginning of the next row, then work 4 rows on the remaining 4 sts. Cast off.

Join wool to armhole edge of right front shoulder, and work to correspond with other front.

Sleeves

Cast on 24 sts and knit 4 rows.

Work 10 rows in st st.

Continue in st st, inc 1 st at both ends of the next row and every following 6th row until 3 inc rows have been worked (30 sts).

Work 3 rows straight.

To shape sleeve top:

Continue in st st, dec at the beginning of each of the next 8 rows. Cast off.

Work a second sleeve the same.

Neck edging

First join shoulder seams. With wrong side of work facing, pick up and knit 42 sts from all around the neck edge.

1st row: k1, *k2 tog, repeat from * until 1 st remains, k1.

2nd row: k1, *pick up 1, p1, repeat from * until 1 st remains, k1. Cast off.

To make up

Press on the wrong side as previous garments. Join the sleeve seams, and carefully set the sleeves into the armholes. Thread ribbon through holes at neck.

Bonnet

Using coloured wool and 2.75 mm (12) (US 2) needles, cast on 44 sts for the face edge.

Knit 4 rows, working into the back of the sts on the first row to give a neat edge.

Change to 3.25 mm (10) (US 4) needles.

Knit 1 row and purl 1 row.

Work in pattern as follows:

1st row: k2, *k1, p2, repeat from * until 3 sts remain, k3.

2nd row: k2, purl until 2 sts remain, k2.

3rd row: k2, *p1, k2, repeat from * to end.

4th row: As 2nd row.

Repeat the last 4 rows twice more, then repeat the 1st and 2nd rows once.

Continue in st st with a k2 border at each end of every p row for 10 rows.

To shape crown:

1st row: k5, *k2 tog, k4, repeat from * until 9 sts remain, k2 tog, k5, k2 tog (37 sts).

2nd and every alternate row: k1, purl until 1 st remains, k1.

3rd row: k4, *k2 tog, k3, repeat from * until 8 sts remain, k2 tog, k4, k2 tog (30 sts).

5th row: k3, *k2 tog, k2, repeat from * until 7 sts remain, k2 tog, k3, k2 tog (23 sts).

7th row: k2, *k2 tog, k1, repeat from * until 6 sts remain, k2 tog, k2, k2 tog (16 sts).

To make up

Break off wool, leaving a long end to thread in a darning needle; pass through all of the 16 sts left on needle, draw up tightly and fasten off securely. Press as described for the coat. Sew up back of bonnet for 4 cm (1½") from centre back. Sew on ribbons at front. If you wish, turn the first part of bonnet back to make a short brim before sewing on ribbons.

ZIRCON *Illustrated on page 74*

These are two necessary extras in any doll's winter wardrobe. Simply by altering the length of the body and size of the waist, and/or changing the size of the needles and the ply of the wool, a wonderful range of these tiny articles can be produced. Originally given in the booklet Dress Your Dolly in Knitting and Crochet *by Ella Allan, published in Melbourne in 1932.*

Singlet

A simple to knit, quickly finished, broken rib pattern singlet with stretch to fit the doll with that little extra girth.

Materials
25 g (1 oz) 3-ply wool
Pair 4.50 mm (7) (US 7) knitting needles

Measurements
(Using 3-ply Bendigo wool and 4.50 mm needles as given; the size will differ if using 3-ply baby wool or other wools)

Shoulder to hem	18 cm (7¼")
Around underarm (unstretched)	22 cm (8½")

Cast on 35 sts. For larger sizes add 4 sts for each size; for smaller sizes use thinner wool and smaller needles.
1st row: Work in k2, p2 rib to last st, p1.
Repeat this row until singlet is the length you require, approximately 15 cm (6") or varied to suit a particular doll, then in garter st cast off all but the last 8 sts.
Work 18 rows in garter st on these 8 sts. Cast off.
Knit another side exactly the same.
Sew down shoulder straps, one to the back and the other to the front of the singlet.
Sew up sides, leaving enough space for armholes.
Crochet a row of: alt 1 tr, 1 ch (US: 1 dc, 1 ch) around neck, then finish off with shells thus: sl st into 1st tr, *3 ch, 1 tr in same st, sl st into next tr and repeat from * all around. (US: sl st into 1st dc, *3 ch, 1 dc in same st, sl st into next dc and repeat from * around.)
Edge sleeves in the same way.
Run a narrow ribbon through the holes at the neck and tie.

Panties

Although these panties my look a little weird in shape when made, they do fit perfectly. Because they are so simple to knit, a little experimentation with wool sizes and needles will give you a wide range of pants for your dolls.

Materials
Large size
25 g (1 oz) 4-ply wool; Pair 4.50 mm (7) (US 7) needles
Medium size
25 g (1 oz) 3-ply wool; Pair 3.75 mm (9) (US 5) needles
Small size
25 g (1 oz) 2-ply wool; Pair 2.75 mm (11) (US 2–3) needles

Cast on 36 sts and knit 2 rows in k2, p2 rib.
3rd row: k1, *m1, k2 tog, rep from * to end of row, ending with k1.
Work 3 rows in k2, p2 rib.
Next row: Knit.
Next row: k21, turn.
Next row: sl 1, k5, turn.
Next row: sl 1, k8, turn.
Next row: sl 1, k11, turn.
Continue knitting in this way, having 4 more sts on the row each time, until you have the full 36 sts on your needle. (This gives shaping to the back.)
Knit 28 rows in garter st (14 ribs), then begin to narrow for the legs:
1st row: Cast off 2, k34.
2nd row: Cast off 2, k32.
3rd row: Cast off 2, k30.
Work in this way until you have 20 sts left on needle.
Work 8 rows in garter st.
Then inc again by casting on 2 sts at the beginning of each row until you have 36 sts again.
Work 28 rows in garter st.
Work 3 rows in k2, p2 rib.
Work ribbon hole as given at beginning, and work 2 more rows of ribbing. Cast off.
Pick up 28 sts around each leg and work 4 rows of k2, p2 rib. Cast off.
Repeat on other leg opening.
Sew up sides and thread ribbon through holes at waist.

GARMENT LAYOUTS

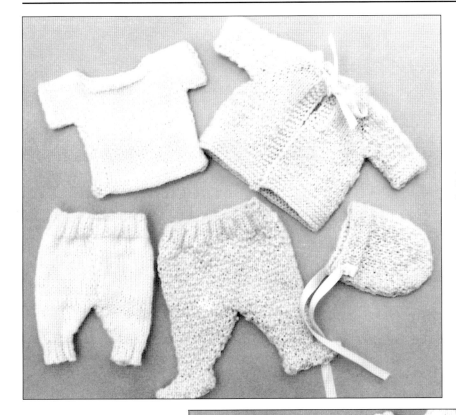

AMBER (clockwise from top right)   Jacket, bonnet, leggings, knickers and vest. Pages 12, 18.

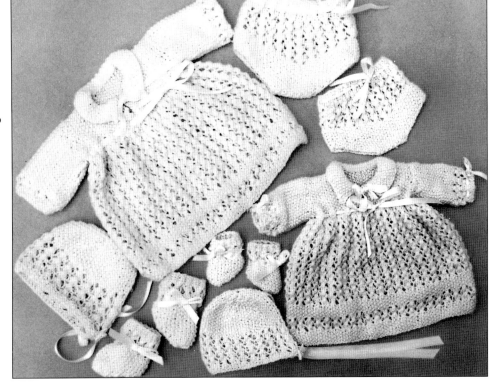

AMETHYST (clockwise from top right)   Panties in two sizes, small dress, bonnets and bootees, large dress. Pages 15, 17.

CARNELIAN (clockwise from top right) Small dress, bonnet and bootees and pants, vest in two sizes, large bootees and panties, large dress and bonnet. Pages 20, 22.

CORAL (clockwise from top right) Petticoat, dress, vest, panties, bootees and bonnet. Pages 25, 37.

DIAMOND (clockwise from top right) Panties, bonnet, dress, vest, matinee jacket and bootees. Pages 19, 28.

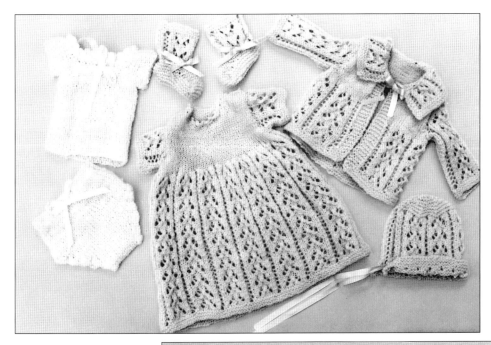

GARNET (clockwise from top right)
Matinee jacket, bonnet, dress, panties, singlet and bootees. Pages 31, 38.

JADE Panties, dress, vest and bonnet. Pages 20, 34.

JASPER (clockwise from top right) Jacket, panties, bootees, vest, dress and bonnet. Pages 36, 39.

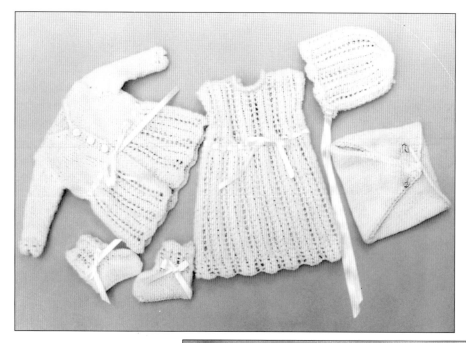

MOONSTONE (clockwise from top right) Bonnet, pilchers, dress, bootees and jacket. Pages 40, 43.

PERIDOT (clockwise from top right) Vest, dress, shoes, combinations, jacket and bonnet. Pages 18, 46.

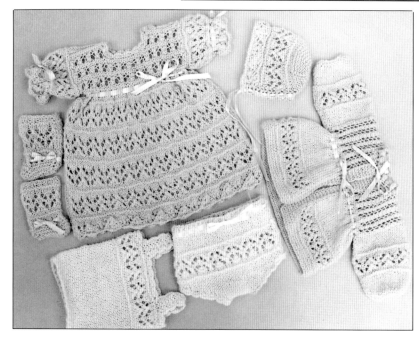

RUBY (clockwise from top right) Bonnet, jacket, panties, vest, bootees and dress. Pages 49, 53.

SAPPHIRE (left to right) Panties, dress, bonnet and bootees. Pages 50, 57.

TOPAZ (clockwise from top right) Dress, panties, vest, patticoats, bootees, bonnet and cape-collared coat. Pages 39, 59.

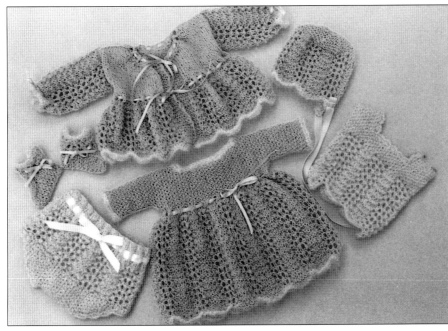

TOURMALINE (clockwise from top right) Panties, bonnet, dress, bootees, vest and jacket. Pages 51, 62.

73

TURQUOISE (clockwise from top right) Jacket, bonnet, dress, panties, bootees and vest. Pages 52, 65.

ZIRCON Vest and panties to suit any doll. Page 68.

BIBLIOGRAPHY

Allen, Ella: *Dress Your Dolly in Knitting and Crochet*, (1932) published by The Speciality Press Pty Ltd, Melbourne
Australian Home Journal (1935)
Australian Home Journal Santa Claus Supplement (1937)
'Cronit' Homecraft Economy Series, No. 318
(*English*) *Women's Weekly* (1938)

Home Budget Toy & Novelty Book (*c.* 1930s–1940s)
Knitted and Crochet Toys, Sydney (*c.* 1930s–1940s)
Knitted Sets for Dolls, Melbourne (*c.* 1930s)
Patons' Craft Book No. 4
Weldon's Practical Knitter No. 462 (*c.* 1920s)

SUPPLIERS

Look in your local phone book under the Craft section if no other classification seems appropriate.

Coats Patons wool is available in most shops specialising in wool, and also in the haberdashery departments of large stores such as Myers, David Jones, Big W and K-Mart.

You may find also wools from England in the 2-ply, 3-ply and 4-ply range in many of the specialised wool shops in the southern states of Australia and overseas. Finer wools such as 1-ply can be obtained from miniature (dollhouse) outlets.

Australian made Heirloom Knitting Wools in 3- and 4-ply available in most knitting wool shops, including Mt Waverley, Victoria.

Bendigo Woollen Mills offer a speedy mail order service to their customers, and take most major credit cards. They will willingly send you a sample card of their wools and the colours available for each ply.

Australia
Bendigo Woollen Mills
Lansell Street,
Bendigo, Victoria 3550
Phone (054) 42 4600 until
April 1997, when it will
become (03) 5442 4600

United States
Bendigo Woollen Mills
PO Box 27164
Columbus, Ohio 43227
Phone 614 236 9112

Miniature Design Co.
PO Box 438
Woodridge, Queensland 4114
Phone (07) 209 5672
For fine knitting needles sizes 14–20 and 1-ply wool in all shades, also 1-ply nylon, crepe and mohair. Mail order.

Mt Waverley Wool Shop
9 Hamilton Walk
Mt Waverley 3149
(03) 9807-3750
Mail order

Craftime Shops
Shop 10B
Tweed Mall
Tweed Heads 2485
(07) 5536-7771
Mail order

INDEX